DATE DUE

MAR 0 2 2019			

Demco, Inc. 38-293

POPE JOHN PAUL II

POPE JOHN PAUL II

A Biography

Meg Greene

GREENWOOD BIOGRAPHIES

GREENWOOD PRESS
WESTPORT, CONNECTICUT · LONDON

Library of Congress Cataloging-in-Publication Data

Greene, Meg.
    Pope John Paul II : a biography / by Meg Greene.
            p. cm.—(Greenwood biographies, ISSN 1540–4900)
    Includes bibliographical references (p.) and index.
    ISBN 0–313–32300–3 (alk. paper)
    1. John Paul II, Pope, 1920– 2. Popes—Biography. I. Title. II. Series.
BX1378.5 .G68   2003
282'.092—dc21
[B]   2002192770

British Library Cataloguing in Publication Data is available.

Library of Congress Catalog Card Number: 2002192770
ISBN: 0–313–32300–3
ISSN: 1540–4900

First published in 2003

Greenwood Press, 88 Post Road West, Westport, CT 06881
An imprint of Greenwood Publishing Group, Inc.
www.greenwood.com

Printed in the United States of America

The paper used in this book complies with the
Permanent Paper Standard issued by the National
Information Standards Organization (Z39.48–1984).

10 9 8 7 6 5 4 3 2 1

Copyright Acknowledgments

    The author and publisher gratefully acknowledge permission to reprint extracts from
MAN OF THE CENTURY: The Life and Times of Pope John Paul II by Jonathan Kwitny
© 1997 by Jonathan Kwitny. Reprinted by permission of Henry Holt & Co. LLC. Every
reasonable effort has been made to trace the owners of copyright materials in this book,
but in some instances this has proven impossible. The author and publisher will be glad to
receive information leading to more complete acknowledgments in subsequent printings
of the book, and in the meantime extend their apologies for any omissions.

Dla mojej matki
For my mother

CONTENTS

Photo essay follows page 71

SERIES FOREWORD

In response to high school and public library needs, Greenwood developed this distinguished series of full-length biographies specifically for student use. Prepared by field experts and professionals, these engaging biographies are tailored for high school students who need challenging yet accessible biographies. Ideal for secondary school assignments, the length, format and subject areas are designed to meet educators' requirements and students' interests.

Greenwood offers an extensive selection of biographies spanning all curriculum related subject areas including social studies, the sciences, literature and the arts, history and politics, as well as popular culture, covering public figures and famous personalities from all time periods and backgrounds, both historic and contemporary, who have made an impact on American and/or world culture. Greenwood biographies were chosen based on comprehensive feedback from librarians and educators. Consideration was given to both curriculum relevance and inherent interest. The result is an intriguing mix of the well known and the unexpected, the saints and sinners from long-ago history and contemporary pop culture. Readers will find a wide array of subject choices from fascinating crime figures like Al Capone to inspiring pioneers like Margaret Mead, from the greatest minds of our time like Stephen Hawking to the most amazing success stories of our day like J.K. Rowling.

While the emphasis is on fact, not glorification, the books are meant to be fun to read. Each volume provides in-depth information about the subject's life from birth through childhood, the teen years, and adulthood. A thorough account relates family background and education, traces personal and professional influences, and explores struggles, accomplishments, and contributions. A timeline highlights the most significant life events against a historical perspective. Bibliographies supplement the reference value of each volume.

INTRODUCTION

For many people, Pope John Paul II, born Karol Wojtyla in Wadowice, Poland, was not only a "Man of the Year" but the Man of the Twentieth Century. His controversial stands on abortion and birth control are well known, as is his demand that priests remain celibate and his refusal to allow women to become priests. There is, however, much more to this pope than his conservative stand on issues of sexuality and gender. Some of his most important and enduring contributions have come in the arena of human rights, in his efforts to reconcile Roman Catholicism to Judaism and Eastern Orthodoxy, and his critique of modernism. John Paul has also made the office of pope more visible than ever before, bringing his message to men, women, and children the world over. Almost everywhere he travels, cheering throngs of people gather to greet him, seeking if only for a moment to stand in the presence of this holy man. Even his detractors, of which there are many, concede that the pope is a formidable adversary who is worthy of respect.

Few individuals have found themselves in the midst of so many of the decisive events that took place during the twentieth century. Fewer still have witnessed some of the blackest horrors of which humanity is capable and have maintained their courage, faith, and hope. Not only has John Paul II been a witness to World War II, the Holocaust, and the Cold War, he was also instrumental in bringing about the collapse of the Soviet empire and the reformation of the Roman Catholic Church. Each of these developments has been critical in making the man and in defining his papacy. As a young boy, the future pope challenged the anti-Semitism of his fellow Poles. As pope, John Paul II worked to reconcile Catholicism and

Judaism and to clarify both the failures and triumphs of the Church during the dark years of World War II. At the same time, he continued the relentless battle, begun as a young priest, against Marxism, communism, and any other ideology, including capitalism, which threatened to rob men and women of their dignity and humanity.

To understand John Paul II, it is important not only to understand his times, but also the place with which he most closely identifies: Poland. The history of Poland in the twentieth century is a story of loss, recovery, conflict, tragedy, renewal, and hope. In these respects, Polish history mirrors the life of the pope. Expressing his deep love for, and intense loyalty to, his homeland, the pope told a journalist in 1993, "I have carried with me the history, culture, experience and language of Poland. Having lived in a country that had to fight for its existence in the face of the aggressions of its neighbors, I have understood what exploitation is. I put myself immediately on the side of the poor, the disinherited, the oppressed, the marginalized and the defenseless."[1]

Poland is an old country, dating from the tenth century when six tribes unified to form a single kingdom. Almost from the beginning, Poland has also been subject to conquest and occupation. The Germanic tribes and the Russians posed a constant threat. Yet, the Poles have held fast to their heritage and legacy, and in the process have fostered a determination to be independent and free. Woven into the fabric of Polish history is the Roman Catholic Church. The official state church of Poland, the Catholic Church has remained for many Poles a bastion of strength and a beacon of hope in troubled times. This intensely personal relationship Poles have with their nation and their church has endured for centuries. This unifying sense of nationalism and Catholicism has also had unsavory results, breeding a powerful anti-Semitism that brought ongoing discrimination and recurring violence against the Jews.

Born in the years immediately following World War I, Karol Wojtyla came of age in a world dominated by uncertainty, fear, and hatred. World War I had devastated Europe, claiming nearly ten million lives. The war also destroyed the belief in progress, which had dominated European thought since at least the end of the eighteenth century. Instead of anticipating an orderly and prosperous future, the generation that had survived the war marveled at the extent of human irrationality and ruthlessness. The French writer Paul Valéry (1871–1945) captured this mood of doubt and anxiety when he declared: "We, modern civilization, know that we are mortal. We realize that a civilization is as fragile as a life."[2] The disorder that followed from the war, the growing fear of worldwide communist revolution, and the demoralizing international depression of the 1930s led to the rise of totalitarian governments throughout Europe. All promised to restore stability and prosperity to their nations, but at the cost of freedom.

By the end of World War I, Poland was free, but just barely. During the war, Poland had served as a pawn in the battles between Russia and Germany. Although a Polish Republic was established at the end of the war in November 1918, and although the President of the United States, Woodrow Wilson, called for a "free and independent" Poland in his peace proposal, the country was still menaced by the Soviet Union. Tensions between Poland and Russia led to war in the spring of 1919, but the conflict lasted only seven months. At the time of Karol Wojtyla's birth in 1920, his homeland was enjoying a relatively peaceful interlude as an independent nation, a period that was to continue for only twenty years.

With the invasion of Poland by Nazi Germany on September 1, 1939, the country once more plunged into war and Poles again found themselves at the mercy of a foreign power. Under the leadership of Adolf Hitler, Germany had embarked upon the mission that Hitler believed was the historic destiny of the nation and its people. The modern Germans, in Hitler's view, were the "master race," descended from the mythical Aryans. They must, therefore, be permitted to spread their superior culture throughout Europe and to acquire *Lebensraum* ("living space"). To rid the world of evil, the Germans had the right to conquer and eliminate all racially inferior groups such as the Slavs, the Poles, and, of course, the Jews, whom they regarded as little more than inferior specimens of humanity, fit only for service as slaves to the Third Reich.

By 1942, the Nazis ruled nearly all of Europe, and had initiated a reign of terror almost incomprehensible in the extent of its horror. In Eastern Europe, primarily in Russia and Poland, the dreaded gestapo and *Schutzstaffel* (SS) arrested and executed professors, writers, and priests. Against the Jews, the Nazis waged a war of extermination, a task that they undertook with a rare blend of ideological fanaticism and bureaucratic efficiency. The Nazis began writing what Hitler regarded as a "glorious page" in German history late in 1941 when they expelled from their homes Jews living in German-occupied territories, herded them into walled ghettos, and required them to wear the Star of David on their clothing as an identifying mark. At the Wannsee Conference held in January of 1942, Nazi leaders decided to deport Jews to special camps in which they were to be systematically, efficiently, and economically put to death. Now, Poland was not only a prime source of slave labor, but it also became home to the death camps. The Nazis built no fewer than nine camps in Poland, including two of the most notorious, Treblinka and Auschwitz-Birkenau, the latter of which was located not far from the pope's hometown of Wadowice.

The Holocaust is a crime without historical precedent. Between 1941 and 1945, the Nazis killed an estimated 6 million Jews, 1.5 million of them children. This number constitutes approximately 67 percent of the Jewish population of Europe. The role of the Roman Catholic Church in the Holocaust has long been a matter of controversy. Did the Church do all that it could to save the Jews? Did Catholic leaders, including Pope Pius XII (1876–1958; reigned as pope, 1939–1958), collaborate with the Nazis to help rid Europe of the Jews because of a deep-seated Catholic anti-Semitism? Clearly some did. The president of Slovakia, a Catholic priest named Josef Tiso (1887–1947; president, 1938–1945), willingly gave up Jews to the Nazis when, and sometimes before, they insisted that he do so. In a report prepared on Tiso for the Vatican, Monsignor Giuseppe Burzio reported to the pope that he could find in Tiso "no sign of comprehension, not even one word of compassion for the persecuted."[3]

As pope, John Paul II inherited this troubled legacy. Yet, long before he ascended to the papacy, the Holocaust had left a deep impression on him. For Wojtyla , the destruction of the Jews was never an abstract, historical tragedy. It was personal. Intimately tied to the history of his country as well as his church, the Holocaust had to be confronted. In many ways John Paul II devoted his papacy to addressing the frightful legacy of the twentieth century. He appealed especially for reconciliation with the Jews, apologizing for past errors and reminding Catholic and Jew alike of the ancient connections that linked their two faiths. His was an effort not to forget the past, but to permit old wounds to begin to heal.

The pope has confronted other demons as well. With the defeat of Germany in World War II, Poland's old enemy, the Soviet Union, sought to expand the territory in Eastern Europe under its control. By simply refusing to leave the countries they had helped liberate from Nazi control, the Soviets forced a new master onto Eastern Europe. Karol Wojtyla's beloved Poland fell behind the Iron Curtain. As an avowed enemy of the Communists, Wojtyla was determined one day not only to drive the Russians from Poland but also to destroy communism itself. Throughout his career as a priest, bishop, archbishop, and cardinal, he battled Communist authorities in Poland. As pope, he worked with the Polish resistance movement to defeat the Communists, and in the process helped to inspire a widespread rebellion against Soviet rule, which culminated in the collapse of the Soviet Union in 1991.

In this book I have sought to explain how Karol Wojtyla became the man that he is. I have concentrated on his formative years and his life before he became John Paul II and this allows us to understand the character of his papacy. Karol Wojtyla never imagined becoming pope; his life was not a rehearsal for the high office that he came to occupy. Yet at the same time, his deep curiosity, his desire to learn, his passion for acting and the theater, his athleticism, and his love of the outdoors have proved defining characteristics of his papacy. His many brushes with history, his experiences during World War II, the Nazi occupation of Poland, the Holocaust, and the Soviet occupation of Poland, have all helped shape his temperament and his worldview. Pope John Paul II did not simply emerge with his election to the papacy in 1978; he brought with him to the office an unusual and unconventional background that enabled him to lead the Church into the new millennium while not losing touch with its past.

The dual purpose of this biography is, first, to describe for students the life of the man who became Pope John Paul II and, second, to explain the accomplishments and limitations of his papacy. There is no shortage of material. Not only has the pope been the subject of several long and detailed biographies, he has also published his own reflections on the church and the times. Moreover, as a public figure, he is often in the news, and although aged and ill, the pope still remains one of the most fascinating and most newsworthy individuals in the world.

Had he never even become pope, Karol Wojtyla would still have lived a remarkable life in an extraordinary time. Yet, he did come to sit upon the throne of St. Peter, and his papacy has been one of the most important in the recent history of the Church. Some of the pope's many biographers assert that he has been the most significant pope since the Protestant Reformation and the Catholic Counter Reformation of the sixteenth century. As of 2003, John Paul II has governed the Roman Catholic world for twenty-five years, one of the longest papal reigns in the twentieth century. The first non-Italian pope in 455 years, he has guided the church into the twenty-first century, when the world has again entered an age of uncertainty, fear, and hatred. From the outset, his message has been unwavering: "Be not afraid!" That exhortation, wrote John Paul in *Crossing the Threshold of Hope*, was "*addressed to all people,* an exhortation to conquer fear in the present world, as much in the East as in the West, as much in the North as in the South."[4] No religious leader in the contemporary world, perhaps with exception of the Dalai Lama, has inspired such devotion or commanded such respect. "What ever else one might think," wrote one observer, "the pope deserves our respect as a bastion of uprightness and integrity in a world that is undergoing a crisis of moral leader-ship."[5] Despite the infirmities of age and the ravages of disease, John Paul II has steadfastly continued his mission to carry a message of peace, hope, and love not only to the Catholic faithful but also, and especially, to the lonely, the weak, the downtrodden, the poor, and the suffering peoples of the earth.

NOTES

1. John Elson and Greg Burke, "Lives of the Pope," *Time*, 26 December 1994, p. 60.

2. Quoted in Hans Kohn, "The Crisis of European Thought and Culture," in *World War I: A Turning Point in Modern History*, ed. Jack Roth (New York: Alfred A. Knopf, 1967), p. 28.

3. Quoted in John Lukacs, *The End of the Twentieth Century and the End of the Modern Age* (New York: Ticknor and Fields, 1993), p. 205.

4. John Paul II, *Crossing the Threshold of Hope*, edited by Vittorio Messori (New York: Alfred A. Knopf, 1994), p. 219.

5. Douglas Johnson, "Heaven and Earth through the Eyes of the Pope," *Washington Post*, 21–27 November 1994, national weekly edition, p. 35.

TIMELINE

1920   Karol Jösef Wojtyla is born in Wadowice, Poland, May 18
1926   Begins elementary school
1929   Mother, Emilia Wojtyla, dies April 13
1930   Enters secondary school
1932   Oldest brother, Edmund Wojtyla, dies
1934   Begins appearing in local theater productions
1938   Graduates from high school, moves with father to Kraków and begins classes at Jagiellonian University
1939   Completes first volume of unpublished poetry, *Renaissance Psalter;* World War II begins with invasion of Poland
1940   Meets Jan Tyranowski, who introduces Lolek to the "Living Rosary;" completes two plays, *Job: A Drama from the Old Testament* and *Jeremiah: A National Drama in Three Acts*, and begins working at the quarry
1941   Father, Karol Wojtyla, dies February 18; begins work at the Solvay chemical plant and begins acting in the Rhapsodic Theater
1942   Begins secret seminary studies to become a priest
1944   Struck by a truck and hospitalized; Archbishop Sapieha begins underground seminary at his residence
1945   Germans retreat from Poland, World War II ends, but Soviet occupation of Poland begins
1946   Ordained a priest on November 1; leaves for graduate studies in Rome

1948   Completes first doctorate; returns to Poland from Rome; moves to Niegowić to assume duties as parish priest

1949   Moves to St. Florian's in Kraków

1950   Poem "Song of the Brightness of Water" published pseudonymously

1951   Begins two year academic sabbatical at Jagiellonian University

1954   Appointed to the philosophy department at the University of Lublin

1956   Heads chair of ethics in philosophy department at University of Lublin

1958   Appointed Auxiliary Bishop of Kraków

1960   Play *The Jeweler's Shop* published pseudonymously; book *Love and Responsibility* is published

1962   Vatican II, under the leadership of Pope John XXIII, opens in Rome; speaks on a number of issues at council meetings

1963   Appointed Archbishop of Kraków

1967   Created Cardinal by Pope Paul VI

1968   *Humanae Vitae* issued

1969   Makes first trip to North America, visiting Canada and the United States; institutes Archdiocesan Institute of Family Studies in Kraków

1978   Elected Pope October 16

1979   First encyclical *Redemptor Hominis* is issued; makes first pilgrimage to Poland

1980   Rise of Solidarity trade union and movement in Gdańsk, Poland, shipyard; first visits to Africa, West Germany

1981   Shot in St. Peter's Square May 13; martial law declared in Poland by President Jarulzelski

1983   Second visit to Poland and first visit to Central America

1987   First visit to the United States as Pope, third visit to Poland

1989   Receives Soviet leader Mikhail Gorbachev at the Vatican, visit leads to establishing of formal diplomatic relations between the Vatican and the U.S.S.R.; first World Youth Day held in Rome

1990   Fall of the Soviet Union

1991   Fourth visit to Poland

1992   Public presentation of the official *Catechism of the Catholic Church*

1993   *Veritatis Splendor*, an encyclical on the Church's moral teaching, issued

1994   Book *Crossing the Threshold of Hope* published; Vatican estab-
        lishes "official relations" with the Palestinian Liberation Organi-
        zation and with Israel; named *Time* magazine's "Man of the Year"

1995   *Evangelium Vitae*, an encyclical on the value of human life, issued

1996   Memoir *Gift and Mystery* published; does away with 800-year-old
        tradition in voting for popes by declaring that an absolute major-
        ity instead of a two-thirds plus one will determine who becomes
        next pope

1997   Official Web site of the Vatican opens; more than 2.9 million hits
        are recorded in the site's first three days

1998   First Papal visit to Cuba; celebrates twentieth anniversary of his
        papacy with outdoor Mass in St. Peter's Square

2000   Visits the Holy Land

2001   News reports announce Pope suffering from Parkinson's disease

2002   Responds to priest sex-abuse scandal; visits Toronto for annual
        World Youth Day; makes plans for visit to Poland

Chapter 1

A SON OF POLAND

Young Karol Wojtyla grew up between heaven and hell. Not far from his hometown of Wadowice, an old, provincial Galician village situated near the Skawa River in the foothills of the Beskidy Mountains, is the shrine of Kalwaria Zebrzydowska. There, in 1595, the wife of a Polish nobleman named Zebrzydowska claimed to have seen a vision of Jesus on the cross. To honor his wife's inspiration and to praise God, her husband reconstructed at Kalwaria Zebrzydowska the various places in Jerusalem where Jesus spent the day before his crucifixion. Dedicated to the passion of Jesus and to the life of his mother, the Virgin Mary, Kalwaria Zebrzydowska was famous for an annual outdoor passion play that attracted hundreds of thousands during Holy Week.

To commemorate the journey of Jesus to Calvary, Roman Catholics frequently traveled to Jerusalem to retrace his footsteps. The creation of Kalwaria Zebrzydowska offered Poles an opportunity to participate in the drama of the passion without leaving their own land. Returning again and again to this idyllic and holy spot, Karol Wojtyla doubtless contemplated the meaning of the sacrifice that Jesus had made for humanity, and perhaps here first heard the call to become one of his servants on earth.

Seventeen miles north of Wadowice was the town of Oswiecim, which was long noted as home to both an imperial garrison of the Austrian Empire and a large distillery owned by the family of Jerzy Kluger, who became one of Karol Wojtyla's closest friends. Yet, in 1940, the history of Oswiecim changed forever when Richard Gluecks, an officer in the Nazi army (the Wehrmacht) selected it as the site of a so-called "quarantine camp" to house slave laborers and, more important, to carry out Nazi leader Adolf Hitler's "Final Solution," which entailed the extermination of European Jewry and other "undesirables." The Nazis gave the town the German name by which it is still known: Auschwitz. Karol Wojtyla lived between heaven and hell, and throughout his long life he has come to know the blessings of the one as well as he knows the horrors of the other.

HOME TO A POPE

Wadowice is an old town founded sometime during the middle of the thirteenth century. Those who do not know the history of the place may find it singularly unremarkable. At first glance, there seemed nothing special about Wadowice. Incorporated into the Kingdom of Poland in 1564, along with the rest of the Duchy of Oswiecim, Wadowice, by the early nineteenth century, had become a regional capital in Galicia. Located in the part of Poland then under Austrian rule, Wadowice was indeed modest when compared to the other great cities of the Hapsburg Empire, such as Venice, Prague, Budapest, and, of course, Vienna. Yet Wadowice was no mere backwater languishing outside the mainstream of imperial life and culture. During the early nineteenth century, a garrison of Austrian troops quartered in Wadowice, which, in the minds of many inhabitants, bestowed prestige upon the town and, more practically, enhanced local revenues.

Wadowice enjoyed a measure of economic importance in other ways as well. Growing into a small manufacturing center, Wadowice had a factory that produced steel parts for machines, a steam-powered sawmill, two brickyards, and a plant that made fertilizer from animal bones by treating them with sulfuric acid. There were also two biscuit factories, one of which produced the unconsecrated communion hosts (*oplatki*) traditionally consumed in Polish homes on Christmas Eve.

Socially and culturally, Wadowice thrived, especially in comparison to the impoverished Galician countryside that surrounded it. A small professional class, composed of businessmen, lawyers, merchants, craftsmen, military officers, and government officials, emerged to dominate social and cultural life. As a consequence, by the early twentieth century, the town boasted two restaurants, three public libraries, a gymnastic society, numerous state and private academies, a cinema that showed movies, and a theater often filled to capacity for the performances of local amateur theater groups. In 1922, the most famous of the many literary societies in Wadowice, Czartak, came into existence.

By the early 1920s, Wadowice had grown to almost 10,000 residents. Although horse-drawn carriages remained the preferred mode of transportation, at least six persons owned automobiles. Wadowice was also among the first towns in Poland to be wired for electricity, a process that began as early as 1907. Nevertheless, despite the economic, social, and cultural ferment that characterized Wadowice, and despite the appearance of such modern innovations as movie theaters, automobiles, and electric lights, religion continued to dominate the life of the town and its citizens. The spires of several churches soared above the solid one- and two-story buildings that constituted the major architectural style of Wadowice, while two monasteries and two convents further testified to the enduring religious devotion of the Polish people.

The focus of public worship in Wadowice was St. Mary's Catholic church. Located at the end of the town square, St. Mary's, spreading out beneath an ornate onion dome that was a typical feature of many churches in Eastern Europe, had been a landmark for more than six hundred years by the time Karol Wojtyla was born. Inside, a number of small side altars, each dedicated to a particular saint, flanked an elaborate central altar. In the baptistry chapel, where parents brought their children to be baptized into the Catholic faith, hung a copy of one of the great national treasures of Poland: the "Black Madonna," which Catholic historians believe was painted by St. Luke. The pews at St. Mary's could comfortably accommodate 200 persons, though it was common for the aisles and the vestibule to be overflowing at Mass on Sundays and holy days of obligation.

Although overwhelmingly and devoutly Roman Catholic, Wadowice was also unusually diverse. Perhaps as much as thirty percent of the local population was Jewish, a large number by Polish standards. Most of the Jewish residents of Wadowice and its environs were of German descent, their ancestors having come to Poland as early as the fourteenth century to escape persecution. In a country where anti-Semitism was often prevalent, the non-Jewish residents of Wadowice appear to have been comparatively accepting of their Jewish neighbors, many of whom prospered in commerce, banking, medicine, and law. Although Wadowice did not completely escape anti-Semitic attitudes, tolerance seems to have to out-weighed prejudice, as Wojtyla's recollections confirm. "The Jews gathered every Saturday at the synagogue behind our school," he wrote. "Both religious groups, Catholics and Jews, were united...by the awareness that they prayed to the same God."[1]

THE PERILS OF HISTORY

Into this tangled and at times unsettling world of tradition and innovation, secular ambition and religious devotion, Catholicism and Judaism, to say nothing of international turmoil and war, Karol Wojtyla was born on May 18, 1920, almost at the same time that Poland itself was restored to the map of Europe. For nearly 125 years, Poland did not exist as a country. Since the eighteenth century, Poland had been the plaything of its more powerful European rivals, invaded, conquered, divided, and ruled at various times by Russia, Prussia, and Austria. In 1918, however, at the end of the First World War, U.S. President Woodrow Wilson called for "a free and independent Poland." Concern for the future of the Polish state and nation was one of the Fourteen Points that Wilson put forth as a blueprint for the establishment of a more stable, peaceful, and democratic world. Although the representatives of France, Great Britain, and Italy, the nations that, along with the United States, had defeated the Central Powers, rejected many of Wilson's proposals, this recommendation survived and found its way into the treaties that brought the war to a close.

No sooner had Poland recovered its independence, however, then the nation and its people got their first lesson in the distasteful requirements of international politics. During the peace talks, which were taking place at the Palace of Versailles near Paris, Allied leaders decided to permit the Russians to keep all the territory the tsars had accumulated, including lands in eastern Poland that the Poles wished to reclaim. The Allies' decision was rife with irony. In 1917, the Russian government they now rewarded had toppled Tsar Nicholas II from power and destroyed the Romanov dynasty. Following this revolution, the Bolsheviks, the faction within the Russian Communist party that had seized power, promptly abandoned the alliance against Germany and Austria-Hungary and signed a separate peace treaty with the Germans. The Allies, of course, had no desire to assist the new Russian communist regime. They instead anticipated that the enemies of Bolshevism would eventually triumph, and they sought to leave the country intact for those they hoped would one day inherit it. The Poles would simply have to content themselves with what the Allies gave them.

But the Poles were discontented, and nothing could appease their frustration and anger. In defiance of the Allies' verdict, several Polish groups pledged to recover their former territories, even by going to war if necessary. Arguing among themselves about which group had legitimate political authority, however, impeded their efforts to forge national unity. Not until the Germans released Field Marshal Josef Pilsudski from prison on November 10, 1918, and transported him to Warsaw did the Poles have a leader capable of uniting the competing factions.

Immediately placing Poland under military rule, Pilsudski was mainly intent on restoring order and preventing a Russian invasion. By 1920, though, the situation had changed. Insulted by the treatment Poland had received from Allied leaders, Pilsudski declared war on Russia in an effort to regain the territory his country had lost in the peace settlement. Fighting a Soviet Red Army exhausted by two years of civil war against anti-Communist forces and their Western allies, Polish troops easily seized Kiev, the capital of the socialist republic of Ukraine. V. I. Lenin, the leader of the Soviet Union, had initially advocated Polish independence but was now outraged at Pilsudski's belligerence. With the support of the Ukrainians, who, for the time being, feared the Poles more than the Russians, the Red Army regrouped and recaptured Kiev in May.

On the day Karol Wojtyla was born, Lenin, along with the future leader of the Soviet Union Josef Stalin and the Soviet Minister of Defense Leon Trotsky, were debating their next move. They ordered an invasion of Poland, determined once more to conquer and rule it. Within days of Karol Wojtyla's baptism, which took place on June 20, 1920, in a small church on the town square of Wadowice, the Red Army was driving toward the Vistula River, only 180 miles to the northeast. With Soviet troops advancing on Warsaw, the Polish capital, Pilsudski solicited aid from the victorious Allies, but the war-weary French and British and the increasingly isolationist Americans declined to help. A message read from the pulpit of every church in Poland called all young men to their duty, and volunteers flooded Warsaw eager to defend their country. With the Red Army in disarray as its commanders bickered over the plan of attack, the Poles managed to check the Russian assault and send the Soviets fleeing for the safety of their borders.

The Poles credited their triumph, which they termed "The Miracle of the Vistula," to the intercession of the Virgin Mary. Pilsudski, though, had less exalted, more worldly ambitions: he wanted to punish the Russians further and so once again attacked Ukraine. After months of combat, the two sides fought to a bloody stalemate and negotiated an armistice that reestablished the original boundary that had existed before the slaughter began.

Although the Poles were proud of having prevented a communist takeover of their country, the victory they had won hardly solved all their problems. The Communists still ruled the Soviet Union, and the threat that communism would spread and engulf the rest of Europe seemed real. "In a year," Trotsky had proclaimed in 1919, "all Europe will be Bolshevist."[2] German communists, after all, had demonstrated their strength by capturing Munich, if only for a brief time. Their success, not surprisingly, inspired imitation. It also kindled the wrath of a disillusioned veteran of the First World War named Adolf Hitler, who was growing ever more resentful about German defeat and humiliation, which he vowed one day to reverse. Before Karol Wojtyla had reached his first birthday, the dark forces were already gathering that for the rest of the twentieth century would battle for power over nations and grapple for the souls of men.

A CHILD IS BORN

And so, while the world spun toward catastrophe, the parents of the future pope, Karol Sr. and Emilia Wojtyla, welcomed their third child (a daughter died as an infant) and second son into their family. Although Karol was a lieutenant in the Polish army, at 41 he was too old in 1920 to go to the front. He remained in Wadowice, working as an army postal clerk and caring for his wife and his son Edmund, who had been born in 1906. The couple named their new son Karol, the Polish equivalent of "Charles," but called him "Lolek," the equivalent of "Chuck" or "Charlie."

Karol Sr. and Emilia rejoiced at the birth of a healthy son, more so since six years earlier, in 1914, Emilia had given birth to a daughter, Olga, who died within weeks. Emilia never fully recovered from the emotional trauma of the baby's death. A decade later, she told a neighbor that she still "felt sorrow because of the loss of her daughter."[3] His mother's sorrow must also have left a deep impression on Lolek. In an account of his life that he gave shortly after ascending to the papacy in 1979, John Paul II mentioned "the big sister who had died" sixty-five years earlier and six years before his own birth. So the Wojtylas had more than one reason to celebrate the birth of their son. Yet, the delivery had taken its toll on Emilia, further weakening her already frail and tired body and anticipating future problems.

Lolek lived with his parents and his brother at Rynek 2, a crowded second-floor apartment in a building that faced the town square. Their landlord was a wealthy Jewish merchant named Chaim Balamuth whose family occupied the ground floor. Next door to the Wojtylas lived another Jewish family, the Beers, whose daughter, Regina, was two years older than Lolek.

A curving iron staircase led to front door of the Wojtyla apartment, which faced a pretty, walled courtyard and the town square. From the Wojtyla flat, the pope recalled, one could see the stone wall of the Catholic church and a sundial inscribed with the Latin aphorism: "*Tempus fugit, aeternitas manet*" (Time flies, eternity remains). So close did the Wojtylas live to the church, wrote one of the Pope's biographers, that:

> a priest with an average nose would have smelled the family dinner. Unlike the stone basilicas that soar over some Polish villages, the Wadowice church is masonry, and only a few stories high. Nevertheless it cast a physical shadow over the Wojtyla home, and doubtless a spiritual one too.[4]

The apartment itself consisted of three rooms: a living room, a kitchen that doubled as a bedroom, and another bedroom, attached to each other "railroad style." The flat had no bathroom because in 1920 Wadowice had no indoor plumbing or running water. Water for bathing, cooking, and cleaning had to be drawn from one of two wells in the market square.

Lolek Wojtyla descended on both sides of his family from Polish peasant stock, who traced their origins to the eighteenth century. His father was born in Lipnik on July 18, 1879, the son of a tailor. Little is known about him. After completing high school, Karol Sr. studied for an additional three years before returning home to take up his father's profession. In 1900, at the age of twenty-one, Karol was drafted into the Austrian army, embarking on what would become a lifelong military career. He was first posted to Wadowice and later further east to Lwów. Rising quickly through the ranks, Karol was promoted to sergeant in 1904 and put in charge of a platoon. That same year his duties brought him back to Wadowice.

There Karol Wojtyla met Emilia Kaczorowska, the frail daughter and the fifth of thirteen children born to a prosperous Kraków saddlemaker. According to family lore, the two met at church where both had gone to light candles. The delicate and sensitive young woman with a caring and gentle disposition was attracted to the reserved and gentlemanly soldier, and the two wed later in 1904. The disapproval of Emilia's choice of a husband marred the couple's happiness. Maria Kydrynska Kydryński Michalowska, a close friend of the Wojtyla family during the 1930s, remembered that Emilia's parents thought that she had "made a bad choice. They were wealthy bourgeois and didn't like him," believing that their daughter had married beneath her station. [5]

One of the few surviving photographs of Karol and Emilia is their wedding picture. In that photograph, Emilia's small, white-gloved hand rests on her new husband's arm. Karol Wojtyla looks handsome in his military uniform, the three silver stars on each side of his collar indicating his rank. Although not a tall man, Karol had a broad, square, handsome face with dark eyes, short-cropped hair, and a moustache turned slightly upward at each end. In the photograph he appears serious and sober, a description that his army file supported. He was, according to his superiors, "extraordinarily well-developed with a righteous character, serious, well-mannered, modest, concerned with honor, with a strongly developed sense of responsibility, very gentle and tireless at work." Those qualities also included a facility with languages (Karol was especially fluent in Polish and German), an ability to think quickly and well, and the practical and valued ability of being a typist with quick hands.

A year after his marriage to Emilia, Karol earned another promotion to the rank of warrant officer in the quartermaster corps. With the outbreak of the First World War, however, Wojtyla was ordered to the Russian front, where his actions in combat won him the Iron Cross of Merit with Cluster, an honor that recognized him as an unusually brave noncommissioned officer. With the end of the war, the defeat of Germany and Austria, and the emergence of a free and independent Poland, Karol Wojtyla, like many other Polish veterans, enlisted in the Polish army. Assigned the rank of first lieutenant in the 12th Infantry Regiment, Wojtyla returned to Wadowice. Although he did not make as much money as the local merchants and professionals in Wadowice, his rank and occupation afforded the family considerable prestige in the community.

The esteem with which Karol's neighbors regarded him was very much in evidence on June 20, 1920, when a large number of family and friends gathered at St. Mary's Church for the baptism of the new baby. Lolek was formally christened by a local military chaplain as Karol Józef, in honor of his father and the former monarch of the Hapsburg Empire, Frans Józef, that his father had once served. Early pictures of Lolek show a chubby boy with a broad face, whose features bore a marked resemblance, like those of his older brother Edmund, to his mother. Whether because he was her youngest child, or because she was troubled by memories of the infant daughter who had died, Karol became Emilia's favorite. She believed her son to be destined for greatness. One popular story told by friends of the family describes how Emilia put her son in his pram and walked all around Wadowice to show him off to neighbors and strangers alike. A neighbor who on occasion babysat Lolek remembered in particular one instance of his mother's pride:

> His mother used to yell up to us to say, "You will see what a great man will grow from this baby." We all used to laugh at her and say she had a loving heart but could not predict the future. But everyone fussed over him as if he was a prince.[6]

Even as her health continued to decline, Emilia took great delight in fussing over her youngest child. She often read to him, and during the warm spring and summer months sat with him in the courtyard and watched him at play while she sewed. In later life the pope would recall his mother as "heart," whose gentle and loving spirit the whole family cherished.

How miserable it must have been, then, for her sons and her husband to watch Emilia's chronic heart and kidney problems worsen, and to see her slip more frequently into the depths of melancholia from which they could not rouse her. There were days when Emilia, suffering terrible physical pain, closed the door to her room and took to her bed. The closed bedroom door signaled Lolek to stay away from his mother so she could rest. At these times, Karol Sr. assumed the household duties, cooking and cleaning for his sons and his wife. Even when she felt well enough to get out of bed, Emilia suffered from dizziness and fainting spells. Her husband took her to doctors in Kraków in the hope of finding a cure, but nothing they did brought permanent improvement.

A FULL LIFE

Despite Emilia's illness, daily life in the Wojtyla household was quietly happy. Karol Sr., now a quartermaster in the Polish army, left home every day to fulfill his duties at regimental headquarters. Emilia stayed at home, and when she felt well enough, took in sewing to supplement the family income. Lolek's older brother Edmund was a student at the local high school. The Wojtylas were also devoutly Catholic. Images of the saints appeared throughout the apartment, and the family recited morning prayers together before a small altar in the parlor. Karol Sr. even hung a holy water font near the front door so that anyone entering or leaving the apartment could bless themselves. Every evening, the family read aloud from the Bible and said the rosary. On Sundays and holy days of obligation, they always attended Mass.

Lolek's first religious instruction came from his mother, who taught him how to make the sign of the cross. It was his father's faith, however, that made the deepest impression upon him. Karol Sr., the future pope remembered, was a "very religious man…of constant prayer."[7] He often prayed silently on his knees at home and read the Bible with his sons. When Lolek was nine years old, his father took him on his first religious pilgrimage to the nearby Kalwaria Zebrzydowska. Lolek admired his father's piety and tried hard to emulate it. Yet, his father sometimes scolded him for being negligent in his devotion, chastising him more than once for not praying "adequately" to the Holy Spirit for guidance, fortitude, and illumination.

Karol Wojtyla's influence on his son was immense. In passing on his religious beliefs, Karol taught Lolek that the Catholic Church was much more than a religious institution. It also had an "invisible dimension." The church helped to guide the faithful in their earthy lives, but the church itself was merely an instrument. The key to finding God, Karol Wojtyla believed, lay in personal sacrifice and suffering. Years later his son wrote that he was "above all" indebted to his father for his religious upbringing. "We never spoke about a vocation to the priesthood, but *his example was in a way my first seminary, a kind of domestic sanctuary.*"[8] The sense of personal sacrifice and suffering, and the daily practice of spiritual devotion, became important aspects of young Lolek's life, and doubtless sustained him in the trials he was about to experience.

By the time Lolek began to attend elementary school in 1926, Edmund was already enrolled at the university. Although Lolek missed his older brother, he excelled in his classes and soon distinguished himself as a fine student. He also got along well with his classmates and seemed never to quarrel with anyone, a talent he retained in later life when he showed "a knack for dodging the interpersonal disputes that pop up in most people's everyday lives."[9]

But Lolek's boyhood was not filled only with study and religious meditation. He had made friends with a number of other boys, and when not in school or at home, was often engaged in some kind of play or athletic activity. One early childhood friend was Boguslaw Banas, whose father owned a whiskey and snack bar in Wadowice, and a dairy on the outskirts of town. Lolek's parents also enjoyed the company of the Banas; Emilia talked regularly with Boguslaw's mother while the two boys played nearby. Boguslaw later recalled that the usually reserved and reticent Karol Sr.

seemed to warm up around Boguslaw's father who, according to many residents of Wadowice, was his only real friend.

Lolek soon discovered that he enjoyed playing outdoors, thus marking
the start of a lifelong love of sports and outdoor recreation. He played soccer on the school team, though his talent was not considerable. According to one teammate, Lolek was a great friend, but unfortunately a lousy
goalkeeper. In the winter, Lolek and his friends liked to ski in the nearby
mountains, despite the threat of wolves on the prowl. The Skawa River
provided no end of opportunities. During the winter it served as an ice
rink on which to play hockey; in the spring and summer it was ideal for a
refreshing swim. In good weather, Lolek often took long hikes through the
countryside, or climbed trees near a friend's farmhouse. Sometimes Lolek
and his friend Zbigniew Silkowski went to the Silkowski house near the
train station to watch the railway workers.

When the weather at last forced Lolek and his friends indoors, they still
found plenty of activities to amuse them. Karol Sr. read to them from one
of his history books. They also played Ping-Pong at Boguslaw Banas'
house. Even religion entered the boys' play. At the Wojtyla house, the
boys gathered at the makeshift altar in the parlor, and played "priest," a
game that Lolek particularly enjoyed. Dressed in a special cape that his
mother had made for him, Lolek and his friends would "say" Mass, carefully imitating the gestures and prayers they knew by heart from serving as
altar boys at St. Mary's.

Lolek's circle of friends included both Catholics and Jews. His life became an intriguing blend of two distinct cultures: the intense Polish
Catholicism of his parents, and the dynamic Judaism of his friends. At a
time when anti-Semitism was on the rise in Poland and throughout Europe, Wadowice remained a unique haven for Jews. While Lolek's parents
were strict in their faith, they also encouraged their son to learn about
other faiths. As a result, he occasionally accompanied his Jewish friends
to their services at the local synagogue. Lolek even volunteered to play for
the Jewish side in soccer games against the Catholics, whenever the Jewish teams were short a player. On one occasion, Jerzy Kluger ran to the
Catholic church where he found Lolek at prayer. A woman remarked how
strange it was to see the son of a Jewish community leader entering the
Catholic church. Overhearing the comment, Lolek asked: "Aren't we all
God's children?"[10]

Lolek had forged a strong friendship with Jerzy Kluger, the son of a
wealthy Jewish family in Wadowice—a friendship that continued
throughout their adult lives. Jerzy's father was a lawyer who practiced law

near the Wojtyla's home. The two boys thus saw each other often, and spent a great deal of time playing together in the town square. As boys have always done, Lolek and Jerzy displayed a great aptitude for getting into mischief. One of their first escapades occurred when they were six years old. Convinced that the town constable, Mr. Ćwięk, had a wooden sword, Lolek and Jerzy tried to steal it one afternoon when they came upon Ćwięk napping in a chair outside the jail. As they carefully eased the sword from its scabbard, they lost their balance and fell. Officer Ćwięk was angrier about having his nap interrupted than he was about the boys try-ing to make off with his weapon.

"IT WAS GOD'S WILL"

On April 13, 1929, while Lolek was in school, his father arrived and asked to speak to his teacher. After a brief conversation, the teacher, Zofia Bernhardt, summoned Lolek from the classroom. She had terrible news: Lolek's mother was dead. Just five weeks away from celebrating his ninth birthday, Lolek saw his former life fall to pieces with all the sudden inten-sity of an electric shock. Bernhardt nonetheless recalled the boy's quiet composure. He replied only "It was God's Will."[11]

Even before her death, Emilia's chronic illnesses had kept her apart from her son, a privation that Lolek felt keenly into adulthood. As pope, he admitted to having "felt deprived whenever his mother left for Kraków in search of another promised cure for her ailments."[12] Toward the end of her life, Emilia also suffered from paralysis in her legs, making her a virtual invalid and a recluse. Because it was considered bad manners at the time to ask about a person's sickness, Emilia must have felt even more isolated and alone. Either because her disease was feared to be contagious or be-cause her doctor thought it essential that she rest and avoid exerting her-self as much as possible, Lolek visited with her infrequently during the last months of her life, and only ever for short periods of time. He was already missing her before she died.

After a funeral Mass at St. Mary's, Emilia Wojtyla was buried. The fol-lowing day, Karol Wojtyla took his sons on a pilgrimage to Kalwaria Ze-brzydowska, where they knelt together in prayer at the great altar in the basilica. Despite his calm demeanor, Lolek was emotionally devastated by his mother's death, admitting to a classmate that he had wept at her grave. When he had grown, he wrote a poem, "The White Grave," to her memory:

> Over your white grave
> White flowers of life bloom—

Oh, how many years have gone by
Without You—how many years?...
Over your white grave
O Mother, my extinct beloved,
For a son's full love,
A prayer:
Eternal Rest—[13]

Karol Wojtyla cherished the memories of his mother, all the more because there were so few of them. In his autobiography, he admitted that he
"does not have a clear awareness of her contribution," though he believes
her efforts in his religious training "must have been great."[14] Emilia's
death, of course, brought about an immediate change in the Wojtyla
household. Karol Sr. alone was now responsible for the care and upbringing of his young son. He did not take his obligations lightly, and during
the next several years, father and son formed a powerful bond that enabled them to master their grief, and that cemented in Lolek the ideals,
values, and beliefs that sustained him through all the trials yet to come.

NOTES

1. George Weigel, *Witness to Hope: The Biography of John Paul II* (New York: Harper Collins, 1999), p. 24.

2. Jonathan Kwitney, *Man of the Century: The Life and Times of John Paul II* (New York: Henry Holt, 1997), p. 29.

3. Kwitney, p. 31.

4. Ibid., p. 32.

5. Ibid., p. 31.

6. Robert Sullivan, *Pope John Paul II: A Tribute* (New York: Time, 1999), p. 11.

7. Weigel, p. 30.

8. John Paul II, *Gift and Mystery: On the Fiftieth Anniversary of My Priestly Ordination* (New York: Doubleday, 1996), p. 20.

9. Kwitney, p. 36.

10. Carl Bernstein and Marco Politi, *His Holiness: John Paul II and the Hidden History of Our Time* (New York: Doubleday, 1996), p. 17.

11. Kwitney, p. 35.

12. Ibid., p. 31.

13. John Paul II, *The Place Within: The Poetry of John Paul II* (New York: Random House, 1994), p. ix.

14. John Paul II, *Gift and Mystery*, p. 20.

Chapter 2

A YOUNG MAN OF PASSION

Emilia's death left a vast emptiness in the lives of Karol Wojtyla and his sons. Perhaps because he had not seen his mother very much during her last illness, Lolek was not only saddened but devastated by her death. He missed her terribly, and in his grief his once carefree nature disappeared. He became more and more withdrawn, seeking solace in study and prayer. The change did not escape Lolek's classmates, several of whom remarked on his deepening melancholy. When anyone asked about his mother, Lolek said merely that God had taken her away. He would say nothing more. On this and other matters Lolek now began to keep his own counsel, refusing to rely on others for help, a characteristic that remained with him throughout his life. Despite his sorrow, though, Lolek still found the time and energy to help his classmates with assignments and to play soccer, and he continued to excel in his studies. Meanwhile, Karol Sr. grieved privately, for with his wife's death he now had a young son to care for.

But time and the world had taken their toll on Karol Wojtyla. His once thick, black hair was almost completely gone, and the neatly trimmed mustache was now little more than a tiny triangle. Although he had retired from the army in 1927 with a modest pension, Karol had continued to work part-time. With Emilia's death, however, father and son had to establish a new rhythm to their everyday lives. Karol wanted his son's life to be as little disrupted as possible, so he always made sure to set aside two hours a day for outdoor recreation. Rainy days might find the two playing a furious game of Ping-Pong at the Catholic house next to the church. On those rare days when Karol was too busy to care for Lolek, neighbors stepped in to help.

Karol, of course, took over many of the household duties, such as cooking breakfast and supper for Lolek and himself. They almost always ate their noon meals at the Banas' restaurant, which provided a small but festive respite from their responsibilities and their mourning, and offered a chance to visit with friends. Lolek took great pleasure in those meals with his father; they afforded him moments of real joy in the midst of the most painful and difficult time of his life. One such occasion, however, was the scene of his first brush with death. A local policeman often stopped into the Banas' establishment to have a drink or two. Whenever he thought he had drunk too much, the policeman removed his gun from his holster and placed it in the cash drawer for safekeeping. When Lolek was almost fifteen, his friend Boguslaw took the gun out of the drawer and pointed it playfully at Lolek, who was standing about six feet away. Yelling "Hands up or I'll shoot!," Boguslaw accidentally pulled the trigger. The bullet narrowly missed hitting Lolek and instead shattered a window. Boguslaw's father, who had been napping, was awakened by the shot. He "burst into the room, took the gun from Boguslaw, and returned it to the cash drawer. No one said a word. Everybody knew it had been a close call."[1]

Lolek spent his evenings listening to his father read from history books to supplement Lolek's education. Jerzy Kluger, who was present for many of these evening readings, recalled that Karol's voice was "low…not dynamic as Karol [Junior's] turned out to be."[2] Karol also tried to teach his son German, though his efforts were not successful. When he was not working, Karol busied himself cooking, cleaning, washing, and even darning socks. He also used his skills as a tailor to mend Lolek's clothing, from time to time altering his old military uniforms so that his son could have "new" pants and shirts for school. Janina Kotlarczyk, the sister of Lolek's high school drama teacher, recalled once how Lolek's father took a green military coat that had belonged to him, and made Lolek a new coat out of the old one. Lolek's friends teased him about this coat, calling him "Karol of the Green Coat."[3]

Although the everyday routine was necessarily rigid, Lolek seemed to flourish under it. Karol's pleasures were few: an evening stroll, perhaps an occasional swim, reading the daily newspaper, and the company of his son. But the days were not filled with only work and prayer, for Karol and his son also enjoyed play. The two loved taking long walks and one could see them most every evening strolling through Wadowice; Sundays after Mass they took even longer walks outside the town or hiked in the surrounding hills. Karol's classmate Zbigniew Silkowski remembered going to the little apartment at 2 Rynek Street. As he approached the front door, he heard shouts coming from inside accompanied by pounding feet. Then someone cried "Gooo-aaal!" Entering the apartment, Zbigniew Silkowski found Karol and Lolek out of breath and covered with sweat. They had been playing soccer.[4]

To sharpen Lolek's soccer skills, Karol and his son played one-on-one soccer matches with a ball made of rags in the small living room of their apartment. Since Emilia's death, the room was no longer of much use. The rugs had been rolled up and the furniture covered, and the room worked perfectly for impromptu soccer matches.

Karol and Lolek did spend a great deal of time in prayer and meditation. The back bedroom of their apartment, which they now shared, contained a small, makeshift altar that Emilia had made. Here Lolek, dressed in the white robe his mother had sewn for him, prayed alone, or in the company of his father before the altar. They also went often to St. Mary's to pray together. Lolek's devotion was growing.

Yet, people still worried about him. He seemed content, but friends, neighbors, and relatives feared that his apparent composure hid the grief that he felt at his mother's death. Would his sadness cripple him, they wondered? Would he recover from his loss or would it poison the rest of his life?

GROWING UP, GROWING OLD

In 1930, Lolek and his father traveled to Kraków to attend his brother Edmund's graduation from medical school at Jagiellonian University. Now twenty-four years old, Edmund had matured into an intelligent and energetic young man with his mother's looks. He was known as an excellent athlete, especially on the soccer field, as well as a formidable opponent in chess. So it was with great excitement that Lolek learned that with his brother's studies now completed, Edmund would work in Emilia's hometown of Bielsko-Biala, which was not far from Wadowice. Lolek eagerly looked forward to Edmund's visits to Wadowice, and to visiting him in Bielsko-Biala, where Lolek sometimes accompanied his brother to the hospital where he worked. Edmund was a talented and compassionate physician, but had not lost his sense of humor or showmanship. He entertained the patients by doing one-man performances in which he read or recited. By all accounts, some of Lolek's light-heartedness and enthusiasm returned with Edmund nearby. Karol was also pleased to have his eldest son near, for not only did he enjoy Edmund's company, but having a doctor in the family meant that the household finances would not be as strained as they had been.

Edmund liked spending time with his father and his younger brother. On his frequent visits home, he played soccer with Lolek, or attended matches with Lolek perched on his shoulders so that he could see above the heads of crowd. Edmund also taught Lolek how to ski, and the two spent hours skiing or hiking.

In addition, Edmund and Lolek shared a love of theater and acting. But Edmund realized that he had to be more than a companion and friend to Lolek. He needed to provide the kind of guidance that only an older brother can give. To that end, Edmund took it upon himself to become a role model for his brother, in an effort to show him "how to use time to achieve as much as possible in life."[5] Edmund's lessons were well taught and Lolek applied them rigorously. Despite the difference in their ages, the two brothers grew extremely close.

By 1932, just as they had learned to deal with the absence of Emilia from their lives, Karol and Lolek learned that Edmund, who had been treating a patient with scarlet fever, had himself fallen ill. After four days of suffering, Edmund died alone in the hospital where he had worked. His death was a cruel blow. Karol had lost not only his wife, but two of his three children. For Lolek, Edmund's death was catastrophic. On the day he learned Edmund had died, a neighbor saw Lolek,

> standing dazed outside the gate to the courtyard of their apartment. 'In a moment of emotion I took him in my arms and hugged him,' she recounts. 'Poor Lolek, you've lost your brother,' she murmured. With a grave face, Karol looked up and said with a resoluteness that left the woman stunned, 'It was God's will.' Then he locked himself up in silence.[6]

Years later, when he had grown to manhood, Lolek's pain at his brother's death lingered. The loss of Edmund was perhaps for Lolek an even greater tragedy given the circumstances under which his brother died. Now more than ever, Lolek turned to his father for solace and guidance. In 1988, as pope, Karol Wojtyla spoke about his father's character and influence on his life:

Almost all my memories of childhood and adolescence are connected with my father. The violence of the blows that struck him opened up immense spiritual depths in him; his grief found its outlet in prayer. The mere fact of seeing him on his knees had a decisive influence on my early years. He was so hard on himself that he had no need to be hard on his son; his example alone was sufficient to inculcate disciple and a sense of duty.[7]

SEARCHING FOR GOD

In January, 1931, ten-year-old Lolek had enrolled at the Marcin Wadowita State Secondary School, an all-boys junior-senior high school, located on Mickiewicz Street. It was the same school that Edmund had attended. At the Marcin Wadowita school, Lolek continued to excel in his studies. When he gathered with other boys after school to play before going home, Lolek invariably excused himself after about half an hour so that he could go to his flat and begin doing his homework. Zbigniew Silkowski described how after he was finished playing he would go to Lolek's house "to copy the Latin homework he [Lolek] had already done."[8] Another former classmate, who came regularly to the flat to study, remembered how after Lolek finished working on one subject, he would excuse himself and leave the room. The classmate, at last unable to control his curiosity, went into the next room to see what Lolek was doing. He found him deep in prayer.

Lolek's piety was by now becoming more and more pronounced; it was apparent that Karol's own example had taken root in his youngest son. In honor of his first communion, Lolek received a scapular, a small woolen badge, from the Carmelite Fathers, which he continues to wear today. Ever since he was ten years old, Lolek stopped every morning without fail in the church across the street from his home to pray for a few minutes, afterward racing to make it to school on time.

When he was old enough, around the time he was nine or ten, Lolek began to serve as an altar boy at St. Mary's where he attended daily Mass. On the days when Lolek served at Mass, his father was always in attendance. Lolek, though, sometimes served at Mass several times a day, happy to take on the extra duties when other boys could or would not. During this period, too, Lolek developed what became a lifelong habit in prayer. Instead of going to the main altar to pray, he prayed at one of the side altars. In this way, Lolek thought, his Catholicism became more intimate, more personal, and thus more meaningful. At St. Mary's, the chapel he favored was the one honoring the Blessed Virgin, no doubt a preference shaped by the memory of his mother. In 1930, shortly after Edmund's graduation, Lolek and his father traveled to Częstochowa to pray before an image of the Black Madonna. It was an experience that Lolek never forgot. In these practices and events originated his special devotion to the Virgin Mary, to whom he dedicated his papacy.

During this period, too, Lolek met a man who exerted a great deal of influence on him. In 1930, Father Kazimierz Figlewicz came to St. Mary's parish. Among his duties were teaching catechism to the parish children. He was also assigned the responsibility of overseeing the altar boys, making sure that at every Mass there were enough boys to assist the priest. One of the boys whom Father Figlewicz became most closely acquainted with was Lolek Wojtyla.

When not hearing his confession or praying with him, the young priest spent hours talking with Lolek. When Figlewicz was transferred two years later to a parish in Kraków, it was Lolek who composed a full page account of his mentor's farewell ceremony for the *Little Bell,* the supplement to the church newspaper, the *Sunday Bell.* Lolek's efforts also marked his debut as a writer. Not only did he quote the entire speech of another altar boy, but he also provided his readers with a detailed account of the ceremony. Almost thirty years later, Karol Wojtyla, then archbishop of Kraków, stated that Father Figlewicz "was the guide of my young and rather complicated soul."[9]

As he grew older, Lolek's devotion to the Virgin Mary also intensified. In December 1935, when he was fifteen, Lolek became a member of the Wadowice high school's branch of Marian Sodality, a national organization made up of Catholic youths pledged to the Virgin Mary. Six months after his acceptance into the group, he was elected president of the Wadowice chapter, an honor that he retained the following year.

Even as Lolek committed himself to Roman Catholicism, those around him did not regard him as "overly religious." One classmate recalled that Lolek never made public demonstrations of his faith, such as crossing himself or praying out loud. Still, none of Lolek's friends dared to swear or tell dirty stories in his presence, respecting the dignity of his quiet convictions. Once when one classmate did sneak up behind Lolek and whisper a curse in his ear, the others seized him and carried him into the bathroom where they beat him. When friends asked Lolek if he were considering the priesthood, he invariably replied in Latin: *"Non sum dignus,"* I am not worthy. Instead, Lolek planned to help solve social problems through the Church, for even then he believed that the Church ought to work hard to achieve social justice.

Lolek's faith did not prevent him from developing a keen appreciation for learning and the sciences. One of his favorite teachers was Father Edward Zacher, a young priest who held doctorates in science and theology. According to another of his former students, Zacher not only taught his pupils how to think, but also that they must be aware in their studies that the search for knowledge never discards God, but encourages one's humility toward Him. Zacher's approach to learning appealed to Lolek's orderly, analytical mind. As pope, Wojtyla encouraged scientific research. He cleared the name and reputation of Galileo, whom Catholic officials had branded a heretic in the seventeenth century because he had concluded, among other things, that the earth was not stationary but moved around the sun.

By the time he had entered high school, Lolek Wojtyla was by all accounts a successful student and popular companion. He continued to make good grades in all of his studies, including Greek, Latin, and Polish, literature, history, and mathematics. Lolek was particularly fond of language, especially Latin, a passion he continued to indulge throughout his life. Lolek made friends easily, though many of the local girls were disappointed when he showed no romantic interest toward them. He enjoyed going to the local cinema, which often showed American films, and spending time at Jerzy Kluger's house where he listened in rapt attention to the classical music played by the local quartet Jerzy's father conducted. On occasion, he was even allowed into the parlor where the group practiced.

Lolek was still passionate about soccer and played for his school team, usually as a goalie. When he was not competing, Lolek and Jerzy Kluger met with other Jewish and Catholic boys to play by the river, where a grassy clearing offered a good playing field and book bags and jackets were used to mark the goals. By this time, Lolek had earned another nickname, "Martyna," after a popular Polish soccer star who also played goalie. Jerzy Kluger recalls that sometimes the games deteriorated into shouting and scuffling matches, with players on the Catholic team yelling "Get the Jew!," one of the few instances of anti-Semitism that he witnessed.[10]

AN IMPORTANT DISCOVERY

In high school, Lolek discovered another passion: acting. He made his first appearance on the stage during 1933, acting in a local outdoor pageant to herald the arrival of summer. Although his role was small and he had no lines, Lolek was captivated by the experience. Over the next two years he appeared in two student productions and also joined the School Drama Circle. A common interest in the theater fostered the growth of a friendship with Halina Kwiatkowska, whose father was principal of Lolek's high school. The two spent many hours together reading and reciting. Lolek even escorted Halina to the senior prom in 1938, which also marked his first formal dance. Although friends often linked their names romantically, the two were never more than very good friends who remain close. In an interview given after Lolek Wojtyla had become John Paul II, Halina stated that "we always played the major romantic male-female parts. That's why it was common thinking [that] we were a couple. He would see me off after rehearsals." But Halina was emphatic that she "never dated him—never."[11]

Lolek's friendship with Mieczyslaw Kotlarczyk, a gifted actor and drama teacher and son of a theater owner in Wadowice, also dates from this period. After college, Kotlarczyk returned to Wadowice where he taught history at the girls' high school and continued to act in the family theater. To Kotlarczyk, "drama was the most important thing in life because it was a way of perfection," and a "means of transmitting the Word of God, the truth about life." He believed that an actor had the power not simply to speak words but to convey meaning that drew an emotional response from the audience. The successful actor functioned much as a priest, opening up "through the materials of this world the realm of transcendent truth." To emphasize his "theater of the inner word," Kotlarczyk staged plays in which costumes, plot, dialogue, and gestures, were stripped to the bare minimum. Kotlarczyk's theories were, for the time, a radical departure from what the theater had been.[12]

Kotlarczyk probably met Lolek sometime in 1935 when Lolek began appearing in amateur high school productions. A year later, Kotlarczyk, impressed by Lolek's talent, took him under his wing. Lolek became a regular visitor to the Kotlarczyk household, where Mieczyslaw tutored him and Halina Królikiewicz. Kotlarczyk's sister, Janina, recalled how her brother paced back and forth in a room while reciting poetry. Walking right behind him was Lolek, who tried to imitate Mieczyslaw's every inflection and gesture, though not always with success. Lolek himself later admitted later that during this time, he was "completely absorbed by a passion for literature, especially dramatic literature, and for the theater." His exposure to the literature of Polish romanticism, which stressed themes of revolution, patriotism, and Catholicism, exercised an incalculable influence on Lolek's thinking as he matured.[13]

The gatherings at the Kotlarczyk home were not always dominated by talk of the theater. Anna Kotlarczyk remembers that Lolek spoke about his life at home. "Being an orphan in his early life, Lolek was trying to find friends and close family," she remembered in an interview. "He felt really lonely after his brother died. And he was growing in theatrical circles." Janina Kotlarczyk recalled that the Wojtylas "were short on money. There was talk that they were poor. But [Lolek] told me that his father was taking good care of him."[14]

For the remainder of his high school years, Lolek immersed himself in theater. Working with Kotlarczyk, he soon became one of the most active and talented performers in the joint high school theater group, the Wadowice Theater Circle. When not performing, Lolek tried his hand at directing. His only setback came in a theater recitation contest in which he won second prize; his friend Halina Królikiewicz took the first place medal. Fifty years later when he and Halina met at the Vatican, he reminded her of their competition, stating, "Yes, I remember that you beat me that time." He later redeemed himself with a spectacular performance in the production of *Balladyna*, a Polish allegorical drama in which he performed in 1937. As is often the case, the drama that took place backstage was almost as intense as the actual production. Two days before the play was to open, the male lead was suspended from school for threatening to shoot a teacher if he received a failing grade. As Halina recalled:

> Lolek suggested quietly, blushing with embarrassment that he could play both roles because the noble Kirkor dies rather early, and he would have time to change costumes to play the ignoble Kostryn. Asked when he expected to learn the second role, Karol replied, 'Oh, I know it already.... I learned it during rehearsals.'... He had a phenomenal memory![15]

Lolek's one known romance came about during the production of *Balladyna*. The character Lolek played falls in love with another character who was played by Kasia Zak, a blonde, blue-eyed, and attractive student at the girls' high school. One day during rehearsals, Lolek was quite dejected. When Janina Kotlarczyk asked him why, he replied that he had just finished rehearsing the love scenes and he admitted to his friend that "I wish it were so in reality!" But when Lolek made known his affection for Kasia, she "laughed, threw up her hands in a gesture of refusal, and cried the Polish phrase *Potrzebuje tego*, which was slang for 'I don't want it.'" According to Janina, Lolek was "crushed" by Kasia's rejection.[16]

Beside participating in local performances, Lolek and other members of the Wadowice Theater Circle traveled to Kraków to see theater productions. The group also gave performances in many local towns. These experiences helped broaden Lolek's education as well as expose him to books and ideas. Many of his friends believed that he was headed for a brilliant career in the theater as an actor. But Karol showed no interest in his son's acting career. No one ever remembers seeing him at any of Lolek's performances. Yet, if Lolek was disappointed by his father's lack of interest, he never showed it.

Lolek's years in high school were some of the happiest he had known. Neighbors remember hearing his cheerful voice singing down the hall as he headed off to school or to rehearsals. He had made a number of close friendships, many of which continued throughout his lifetime. In addition to serving as president of the Marian Sodality, he was also head of the Abstinence Society, which urged young people not to drink or smoke. Lolek was serious about his commitment, but was hardly a fanatic. One day when he and a group of friends were returning from a winter outing, a professor offered the students a bottle of brandy to warm up. One friend noticed that when the bottle was passed to Lolek, he did not hesitate to take a swallow.

Next to his acting, Lolek's other passion during high school was dancing. Twice a month he attended dance lessons held in the Wadowice Gymnasium. Watchful mothers served as chaperones while the boys seated along one side of the gym with the girls opposite them awaited instruction from the local dance teachers. Lolek learned not only how to dance, but the proper way to invite a girl to dance and to escort her to the dance floor. Lolek proved an agile dancer, able to dance every step from waltzes to mazurkas and polonaises. He was invariably polite, but was never shy about asking girls to dance, making him a much desired partner.

Lolek and his friends also enjoyed going to the local Sokol Club to dance to piano and accordion accompaniment. When it came to going to parties, called *pryvatkas,* held at his friends' houses, where boys and girls danced, talked, drank, and flirted, Lolek was nowhere to be found, calling such gatherings a waste of his time.

A GROWING TENSION

By the time he was preparing to graduate from high school in 1938, Lolek was becoming uncomfortably aware of a growing tension not just in Wadowice but throughout Poland. A more pronounced anti-Semitism had emerged after the 1935 death of Józef Piłsudski, the leader of the Second Polish Republic, who had managed to contain anti-Jewish sentiments during his tenure in office. Now economic boycotts of Jewish businesses were becoming more common, and a growing number of newspapers and politicians denounced the Jews. Ginka Beer, who had been one of Lolek's childhood friends, left Poland after an anti-Semitic incident forced her to drop out of medical school. Boarding a train, she warned her friends Lolek and Jerzy Kluger that the horrendous treatment of Jews occurring in Germany would soon spread to Poland. Devastated by his friend's departure, Lolek was too upset to respond, but he feared she might be right.

He already knew that he could not isolate himself from anti-Semitic rhetoric, having performed in a play that denounced Jews. Anti-Semitic violence had already scarred Wadowice. When some local students and teachers joined the anti-Semitic National Democratic party, there was fighting in the streets between Jewish and Catholic Poles. Gangs from outside Wadowice picketed Jewish shops and ridiculed Jewish residents. Many in Wadowice, anxious to maintain the peace, protested these intrusions, but authorities either ignored or dismissed their complaints and the number of anti-Semitic incidents continued to mount.

One night, a mob composed mostly of outsiders stormed through the town, breaking windows in the Jewish businesses and chanting "Economic boycotting is an act of patriotism!" The next day, a number of the townspeople, including Lolek's history teacher, Professor Gephardt, spoke out against the vandalism and violence. After finishing the day's lesson, Gephardt said that he hoped "none of my students are to be numbered among last night's hooligans. I am speaking to you not as a history teacher but as a Pole. What happened has nothing to do with the tradition of our Fatherland."[17] He then told the class about the great Polish nationalist and poet, Adam Mickiewicz, who had throughout his life spoke out for equal rights for the Jewish people. Even Lolek tried to make peace, stressing to his classmates that to be anti-Semitic was also to be anti-Christian. Such efforts at persuasion, however, were fast becoming a lost cause. Lolek began to realize that the world could be an unjust place, but that people, whether Jew or Christian, had a responsibility to fight injustice.

In the shadow of the anti-Semitism that was beginning to descend on Wadowice and Poland, Lolek took his final high school examinations in May 1938. He graduated with a record of mostly A's, stumbling a little in such subjects as chemistry, physics, and history. He made apparent his facility for language when his answers on the Latin exam demonstrated his almost flawless command of that language. His reputation as an excellent speaker and actor helped him win the school's Drama Award; he was also chosen class valedictorian.

Lolek was asked to give a speech to welcome the archbishop of Kraków to a special school ceremony. The archbishop was so impressed with Lolek's presence and speaking ability that he asked the parish priest in Wadowice about Lolek's plans after graduation, hoping that by some chance Lolek intended to enter the seminary. According to one account, the priest answered, "I'm not sure, but it will probably be the university." Lolek then said, "If your Excellency will allow me, I would like to answer myself: I plan to take Polish philology [the study of language] at Jagiellonian University." The archbishop was then supposed to have replied "That's a pity." As Wojtyla later wrote: "I was quite sure that I would remain a layman. Committed, to be sure…to participate in the life of the Church; but a priest, certainly not." Little could Lolek expect that he and the archbishop would cross paths again under very different circumstances.[18] In looking back at that time, though, John Paul II made it clear that:

> In that period of my life *my vocation to the priesthood had not yet matured*, even though many people around me thought that I should enter the seminary. Perhaps some of them thought that if a young person with such evident religious inclinations did not enter the seminary, it had to be a sign that there were other loves or interests involved. Certainly, I knew that many girls from school and, involved as I was in the school drama club, I had many opportunities to get together with other young people. But this was not the issue. At that time I was completely absorbed by a passion for *literature,* especially *dramatic literature,* and for the *theater.*[19]

After graduation, Lolek prepared to enter college the following fall. In the meantime, however, he participated in the compulsory military training required of all young Polish men. On June 20, 1938, he reported to a youth paramilitary army labor battalion. His first assignment was with a road-building crew working in the mountains south of Wadowice. He also spent a lot of time peeling potatoes and serving at Mass. As he had in high school, Lolek made a number of new friends. One of them, Jerzy Bober, who later became a writer and journalist, remembered the first time he met Lolek. Upon coming into his tent, Lolek told Bober "my name is Wojtyla, I am from Wadowice. Call me Lolek." So began another lifelong friendship.[20] Many of Lolek's new companions soon learned not to swear in front of him, intimidated by his quiet demeanor and his commanding presence.

By August 17, Lolek had finished his compulsory duties and returned home. He did not remain long. Karol had decided to move to Kraków where Lolek would be attending university. Later that month, the two packed up their meager belongings and moved to the city. Despite growing up in a small town, Lolek was excited by the change, thinking of all the opportunities a place such as Kraków had to offer a curious, intelligent, and talented young man. Throughout his life, Lolek had been blessed with mentors who entered his life at precisely the moment he needed them. His father, the priests who served his parish, and his drama teacher had all opened to Lolek new worlds and challenged him to become a part of them. Collectively, these men had encouraged Lolek, and instilled in him his patriotism, his love of literature and theater, his philosophical outlook, and most important, his religious faith. He would need all of these resources and more to survive the dark times ahead, for in the same year that Karol Wojtyola graduated from high school and entered the university, Germany annexed Austria and threatened the rest of Central and Eastern Europe.

NOTES

1. George Weigel, *Witness to Hope: The Biography of John Paul II* (New York: Harper Collins, 1999), p. 31.

2. Jonathan Kwitney, *Man of the Century: The Life and Times of Pope John Paul II* (New York: Henry Holt, 1997), p. 36.

3. Ibid., p. 42.

4. Ibid., p. 36.

5. Ibid., p. 37.

6. Ibid., p. 27.

7. Ibid., p. 39.

8. Ibid., p. 36.

9. Ibid.

10. Ibid., p. 41.

11. Ibid., p. 45.

12. Weigel, p. 37.

13. Ibid., p. 33.

14. Kwitney, p. 42.

15. Ibid.

16. Ibid., p. 46.

17. Weigel, p. 39.

18. Kwitney, p. 49.

19. John Paul II, *Gift and Mystery: On the Fiftieth Anniversary of My Priestly Ordination* (New York: Doubleday, 1996), p. 7.

20. Tad Szulc, *Pope John Paul II: The Biography* (New York: Scribner, 1995), p. 82.

Chapter 3

A WORLD TURNED
UPSIDE DOWN

By late August 1938, the Wojtylas were settled in at No. 10 Tyniecka Street, Kraków. Under the staircase of the gray two-story townhouse was a door that led to a tiny basement apartment. The home belonged to Lolek's maternal uncle, Robert Kaczorowski, a leather maker who occupied the main floors with his two spinster sisters. The location, on the south bank of the Vistula River, was superb, providing a majestic view of the city. Nearby was the Debnicki market square, and Lolek could walk to the bridge leading to the old town of Kraków and the university within twenty minutes.

The location and the view, however, did little to make up for the shabby condition of the apartment that Lolek and his father now shared. The apartment was smaller than the one they had occupied in Wadowice. There were two small rooms that Lolek and Karol used as bedrooms, a narrow kitchen, and a bath. Although Lolek's uncle charged a modest rent, a contemporary description left no doubt about the stark accommodations:

> [It] was a sad place indeed. Hardly any daylight filtered through the narrow windows, the rooms were small and cramped, while the lack of sunshine made the place cold and inhospitable. Locals called it the Debnicki "catacomb."[1]

The basement apartment was, in fact, Emilia's legacy to her son. When her parents died, Emilia along with her brothers and sisters had inherited the family home. Her share of the property was determined to be the basement apartment, which had now come into his possession. Lolek had little interaction with his Kraków relatives. When years later he discussed this period of his life, Lolek made no mention of his uncle and aunts, instead describing his father as "his last surviving family member . . . as if the blood relatives upstairs didn't even exist."[2]

Lolek's preparation for classes at Jagiellonian University overshadowed whatever family discord might have existed. One of the most progressive universities in Poland, Jagiellonian had a faculty that was both Catholic and socialist. Whatever their religious and political convictions, all the professors aspired to uphold the school's motto: *Plus ratio quam vis*, "Reason rather than force," and thereby to maintain the school's reputation as a center of Christian and humanist learning. The university also occupied an important place in Polish history, for the noted astronomer Nicholaus Copernicus had attended Jagiellonian during the fifteenth century. Lolek's acceptance to the school was another milestone for the Wojtyla family; following Edmund, Lolek was only the second member of the family to attend college, no small accomplishment for the grandsons of peasants. Going to the university was not only educational for Lolek, it was emotional and spiritual as well. He later wrote that simply walking the paths of the great university could not be done "without due piety."[3]

A DIFFERENT KIND OF STUDENT

Lolek concentrated on the study of Polish philology, that is, the study of Polish literature and language. Housed in one of the many stone and brick Gothic buildings on campus, the Department of Philology at Jagiellonian University was home to several leading scholars. Shortly before classes began in September, however, Lolek got a chance to rekindle his interest in the theater. He was reunited with Jerzy Bober, a friend from military camp. Bober asked if Lolek was interested in helping him plan a drama and poetry reading. Lolek eagerly accepted the invitation. Bober and the other students remembered his appearance on the night that he arrived at the home of Bober's parents:

> Karol's bearing was full of dignity. A new brown hat with a wide band. Instead of regular pants he wore fashionable knickerbockers, and brown shoes of above-ankle cut. A class-

mate remarked that Lolek's hair was uncommonly long, "falling on his neck."

Bober had already warned his companions that Lolek had aspirations to be a poet, though his poetry "was not very understandable." Lolek nevertheless made quite an impression. One young woman recalled that Lolek was "the most distinctive personality there. It was not fashionable to be so different. He talked with grand gestures. He had an open collar—all the other men wore neckties."[4]

Like the other students in the Department of Philology, Lolek "dreamed, breathed, and lived poetry," devoting a great deal of time to composing poems of all types. By the late 1930s, poetry and drama had become two of the most popular literary forms in Poland. This was especially so in Kraków, one of the great Polish centers of literature and culture. The legacy of romanticism and patriotism combined with religion and spirituality to distinguish the work of the newest generation of Polish poets and playwrights. For Lolek, this sensibility, combined with his own intense emotions, inspired a tremendous outpouring of verse and prose that continued well into his papacy. These writings are tremendously valuable in understanding Karol Wojtyla's ideas and emotions, both as a young man, and later as a priest.

Lolek's poetry synthesized his religious beliefs, his mysticism, his devotion to the Catholic Church, and the deep love he felt for his country. As he matured, his poetry began also to address questions of social justice and his growing awareness of the world and its problems. Difficult to read and understand, Lolek's poetry distinguished him from his peers. Later, though, many wondered how he could reconcile his deep devotion to his faith with writing something as frivolous as poetry. As pope, John Paul II answered his critics. The priesthood, he wrote, was not only a sacrament but his life's vocation; writing poetry was simply an expression of his talent. At the same time, he also confessed that "poetry is a great lady to whom one must completely devote oneself; I fear that I haven't been entirely correct toward her."

Given his busy schedule, Lolek must have done most of his writing late at night. By now though, he was in the habit of making the most of every moment. Blessed with an extraordinary ability to concentrate wherever he happened to be, Lolek used his amazing mental and physical strength to carry him through days and nights that would have exhausted most people his age.

Shortly after classes started, on October 15, 1938, Lolek, along with eight other philology students, read a number of his poems as part of a

"Literary Evening in the Blue Room of the Catholic House in Kraków."
The performance was a resounding success as the audience enthusiasti-
cally responded to the students' work. Afterward, with 18 zlotys (approximately four dollars) between them, the student performers decided to
celebrate by going to a popular tavern. According to Jerzy Bober, Lolek's
enthusiasm at the success quickly passed, "Karol—who had already
sobered from the euphoric mood—stopped us with a theatrical gesture.
With a vexed look on his face, he explained that he didn't feel well and
that he was not going to drink or celebrate the event. Hearing this, I
handed him two zlotys, telling him in words brimming with sarcasm,
'Have it Lolek, and buy yourself some candies'.... And Karol, calm as he
could be, brightened up, clutching the coin in his hand and cried 'So long
boys!'" He departed, while the others "astonished...resumed our walk to
the tavern."[5]

When he was not writing poetry, Lolek plunged into his studies. His
first semester was demanding. He was enrolled in courses on Polish ety-
mology (the study of the origins and history of words), phonetics (the
study of the sounds of language made in speech), inflection (the study of
the change in form that words undergo to indicate case, number, gender,
tense, person, or voice), literary interpretation, drama, and the novel. In
addition to his classes, Lolek again became heavily involved in theater.
His performance in the fantasy-fable production of *The Moonlight Cava-
lier*, put on by an avant-garde theater group called Studio 39, so impressed
Juliusz Osterwa, then the leading actor in Poland, that he invited Lolek
and the other actors to his apartment after the performance and told all to
keep in touch. Lolek also joined several student groups that performed poetry, and became a member of the Circle of Scholars of Polish Studies,
which did literary readings. Despite his heavy course load and extracur-
ricular activities, Lolek still found time to study Russian, French, and Old
Church Slavonic, which formed the basis of modern Slavic languages, including Polish. Fascinated by the study of language, Lolek concluded that
without "the mystery of language," neither literature nor culture would
exist. His enchantment with language could easily have steered Lolek toward a career in linguistics, had events not intervened.[6]

Lolek continued to compose poetry. During his first year at Jagiellonian
he wrote lyrics, ballads, and sonnets. Among his works was a cycle of
poems entitled *Renesansowy Psalterz* (Renaissance Psalter), which included the poem "White Grave" written in memory of his mother, and a
drama called "David." The most inspired work from this period is Lolek's
hymn *Magnificat*, which he wrote during the spring and summer of 1939.
In this work, Lolek described his adoration of God, and his appreciation
for the emotions of happiness and sorrow.

Although hectic, Lolek's life in his early student days was also frugal and often solitary. He usually came to and left class alone, saying little to other students. One former classmate recalled that when in class, Lolek listened "as if wanting to soak up every word."[7] Others recall that Lolek, though intelligent and talented, was quiet and appeared less sophisticated and confident than most of his colleagues. The only time he asserted himself was when he felt a Jewish student was being ostracized. He had no use for the Pan-Polish chauvinism, which stressed nationalism and anti-Semitism, that many students and some professors advocated.

By the end of the semester, the fashionable clothing that Lolek had sported was beginning to wear out, and his father had to repair his boots. From time to time, he did meet a few friends for lunch at the student cafeteria, but always made sure that he was home in time to eat evening meals with his father. The two continued their practice of taking evening walks together, during which they enjoyed long discussions about Lolek's courses.

Lolek soon had the reputation of being "different." When attending poetry readings, many students recited the works of friends. Lolek chose to read his own. He always refused to attend the parties held after the readings, usually held at a local tavern. "I have not time to waste on such things," he said.[8] While girls still swarmed around him, he showed no romantic interest in them, and instead concentrated on his studies, his acting, his poetry, and his spiritual life. In apparent exasperation with the seriousness with which Lolek approached life, a classmate one day affixed a card to his desk that read "Karol Wojtyla—Apprentice Saint!"[9]

Time that he might have spent in the company of his classmates, Lolek instead spent with his old friend and teacher Father Figlewicz, who was now stationed in Kraków. Ever attentive to his spiritual life, though still apparently not considering the priesthood, Lolek met regularly with Father Figlewicz.

In June 1939, Lolek took his final exams, earning excellent marks in all classes. To celebrate the end of the academic year, he and some other philology students attended a party. One classmate recalled how "there was some wine and we danced to the [music] of the record player. [Karol] danced like everyone else although he was more passionate about conversation than about dance." That July, Lolek again reported for compulsory military duty. Although granted a student deferment, he still had to participate in a series of exercises held in the village of Ożomla. While there, he helped to build a school and, during off-duty hours, swam and played soccer. In August, after completing his term of service, Lolek returned to Kraków to prepare for the beginning of another semester. Soon those humid late August days along the Vistula seemed to belong to another age.

A WORLD TURNED UPSIDE DOWN

Lolek was in church when the first German bombs hit Kraków. It was Friday, September 1, 1939, and Lolek, as was his custom on the first Friday of every month, had walked to the Wawel Cathedral, the church of the Polish kings, to make his confession and take Holy Communion. His confessor and friend, Father Figlewicz was waiting for him when he arrived. Neither he nor the priest realized that only hours earlier, the *Wehrmacht* ("war maker"), the army of Nazi Germany, had crossed the Polish border at three separate locations in the south, west, and north. The *Luftwaffe*, the Nazi air force, began dropping bombs on Kraków later that morning.

When Father Figlewicz first entered the church, there appeared to be no one there. Thinking that he would not celebrate Mass, he spotted Lolek. "We have to celebrate mass, in spite of everything," Figlewicz told Lolek. "Pray God to spare Poland."[10] The two knelt and began Mass to the accompaniment of the bombs exploding outside. As the stained glass windows of the church rattled and shook, Lolek and Father Figlewicz offered their prayers for deliverance. Figlewicz later wrote that this first wartime Mass, celebrated in the midst of siren screams and the thud of explosions remained forever in his memory.

The invasion of Poland was the latest in a series of moves by Adolf Hitler, the chancellor of Germany, to exert his dominion over Europe. The events that had led up to the invasion, however, were not of great interest to Lolek. While he knew that in September 1938, the Germans had annexed Sudetenland, a region in Czechoslovakia with a large German population, and then in March 1939, had taken over all of Czechoslovakia, Lolek tended to avoid the topic whenever it came up in conversation. One classmate noted that Lolek was more concerned with social issues, such as the growing gap between the rich and the poor, than with the possibilities of invasion and war. When the Spanish Civil War erupted in the summer of 1936, Lolek supported the church stand against the Republic, but otherwise remained vague about his commitments. Although opposed to the Nazis, he seemed at a loss about how to stop them. He believed, as did many Poles, that a German invasion of Poland would never happen, for France and Great Britain would never permit it. The French and the English could control Hitler's demands for territory by diplomatic means, thus making the resort to war unnecessary. Poland would be spared. In a

short time, Lolek's predictions, along with those of most European states-
men, would be proved tragically wrong. Too late, perhaps, Lolek realized
that life as he knew it had changed forever.

That September morning, as soon as Mass was completed, Lolek rushed
home to make sure his father was unharmed. He then helped a friend,
Juliusz Kydryński, drag a cart with his family's belongings to the outskirts
of the city. As they made their way to the edges of Kraków, a flurry of
bombs forced them to stop in the archway of a house. Throughout the ordeal, Lolek stood, silently praying. "Karol remained calm," Kydryński remembered. "Even during the worst explosions we did not exchange a
word. Eventually his calmness spread to me." [11]

The next day, Saturday, September 2, 1939, Lolek and his father also
decided to leave the city and flee eastward, where they believed the Poles
were consolidating their forces and preparing for a counterattack. Joining
tens of thousands of other residents who sought to escape the Nazis, Lolek
and his father took a bus as far as they could, then they began walking. At
one point, they managed to get a ride for a short distance with a truck
driver, but then were on foot again. At last they reached the town of
Rzeszów, located about ninety miles east of Kraków, but were intent to
make their way to Tarnobrzeg, situated on the banks of the San River.

Before they could get to Tarnobrzeg, however, they encountered Soviet
troops who suggested they might be better off returning to their home.
Little did the Wojtylas realize that their flight from Kraków had put them
directly in the path of the advancing Red Army. According to the terms
of a secret agreement signed with Hitler just weeks earlier, on August 23,
1939, the Soviets had invaded Poland from the east on September 17.
Tired and concerned about his father's health, Lolek decided it might be
best to head back to Kraków.

LIFE DURING WARTIME

By September 6, 1939, Kraków was in the hands of the Nazis. In a matter of weeks, all of Poland had collapsed before the Nazi onslaught, known
as the blitzkrieg or "lightning war." Polish soldiers on horseback were no
match for the efficient and deadly Nazi war machine. In the middle of
September, the Polish government sought refuge in Romania. On September 27, the capital city of Warsaw surrendered, and on September 29,
the last Roman Catholic Mass was said at the Wawel cathedral, where less
than a month earlier, Lolek and Father Figlewicz had prayed together
amid the clamor of sirens and the thunder of the bombs. By the beginning

of November, the Germans had annexed the port city of Danzig (now Gdańsk), where the local Nazi leader Albert Forster had announced on September 1 that the hour of deliverance was approaching. The Nazis by then had also seized large portions of western and southern Poland, including Lolek's hometown of Wadowice. Meanwhile, eastern Poland was part of the Soviet zone of occupation. The rest of Poland was a "Nazi colony known as General Government," with the new capital at Kraków. An independent Poland, which had lasted barely twenty years, had once more disappeared from the map of Europe.

"Now life is waiting in line for bread, scavenging for sugar, and dreaming of coal and books," wrote Lolek to a friend in Wadowice during that first terrible autumn of the war.[12] Lolek also mentioned that while a number of his friends had returned to Kraków, several others still had not been heard from. He also noted that the Germans had allowed one theater to remain open, and Lolek and members of his theater group were in the midst of preparing a play.

Lolek, as well as other university students, "were so naive we thought we would be able to complete our studies," explained Lolek's friend Halina Królikiewicz. "On the first day, all the students came to the university, but the Gestapo [the Nazi secret police] surrounded it."[13] Even though they could not attend their classes, Lolek and several other students began to meet in secret with their professors in order to continue their studies. Yet, the worst was yet to come. On November 6, 1939, German officials assembled all the teachers in a meeting where they were placed under arrest and later deported to a concentration camp. Those professors who were taken away were part of a group of more than one million Poles who, for various reasons, ended up in Nazi labor camps where many of them died.

Not only did the Nazis suspend classes at universities throughout Poland, they also closed secondary schools. Nazi officials barred Catholic priests from celebrating the feast days of Polish saints, though they sometimes allowed Mass to be said without a congregation in attendance and with German soldiers standing guard at the doors of the church. (In the Polish countryside, where the Nazis could not fully impose their will, Masses continued to be celebrated, even while the Gestapo kept an eye on potentially troublesome priests who might arouse their congregations to resistance.) Baptizing Jews was strictly forbidden, for the Nazis believed that by this means, Jews might conceal their identities and escape the fate the Nazis had planned for them. Many of the priests, monks, and nuns who concealed or aided the Jews were themselves deported to the camps.

At the same time, the Nazis began a gradual but systematic program designed to eradicate Polish culture. To the Nazis, the Poles, like all Slavic peoples, were something less than human. At the moment, they were useful to the Nazi cause for the labor they provided, and were thus fit to be slaves for the Third Reich. In time, however, they too, like the Jews, would be exterminated. During the occupation of Poland, the Nazis began this process by trying to eliminate all expressions of Polish identity. They closed almost all the theaters, seized priceless art collections, ornaments, and tapestries from museums and private homes, and confiscated invaluable church relics.

The Nazis were intent on wiping out Christianity, which was an essential component of Polish culture. Like the other totalitarian leaders who emerged during the 1920s and 1930s, Adolf Hitler was concerned with the power and influence of religion on national life. Hitler hated Christianity, and could tolerate no faith to rival Nazism. He saw Christianity as a "Jewish swindle," and privately expressed his ultimate intention to destroy all Christian churches and faiths.[14] "The heaviest blow that ever struck humanity," he told members of his inner circle, "was the coming of Christianity."[15]

The Nazi war against Poland thus not only deepened Lolek's recognition of injustice and evil, it strengthened his resolve to defend Christianity as well. He soon came to recognize in Nazism an enemy of all that the Catholic Church taught, believed, and stood for. Lolek essentially adopted what had become the official position of the Roman Catholic Church in 1937. In July of 1933, Hitler had signed the Reich Concordat with Vatican Secretary of State, Father Eugenio Pacelli, the future Pope Pius XII. This agreement established cordial political and diplomatic relations between the church and the Nazi regime. Within a few years, however, the Vatican had become openly critical of the Nazis. Early in 1937, Pope Pius XI issued an encyclical entitled *Mit brennender Sorge* (*With Burning Anxiety*) in which he condemned the treatment of the Catholic Church in Germany. The Nazis, Pius XI declared, had "sown the tares [weeds] of suspicion, discord, hatred, calumny, of secret and open fundamental hostility to Christ, fed from a thousand different sources and making use of every available means."[16] In place of faith in God, the pope concluded, the Nazis had substituted a deification of a race, a people, and a nation.

Lolek agreed with the sentiments of the papal encyclical. He also believed that the salvation of a nation and its people lay not in political doctrines, such as fascism, national socialism, communism, or even liberalism and capitalism, but in Christianity. This philosophy formed the basis for

Lolek's social and political philosophy as a priest, bishop, and archbishop, and was one of the most important ideas shaping his papacy.

For the moment though, Lolek and his father were preoccupied with the struggle to survive. With the Nazi invasion of Poland, payment of Karol's military pension had been suspended, leaving father and son without any means of support. The Christmas of 1939 was, for Lolek and his father, a sad one. Despite the loss of income, the Nazi occupation of Poland, and the disruption of his university studies, Lolek kept busy with his studies and his writings. Like others, he battled with sadness and depression over the Nazi occupation of his country.

During this period, which began in the late fall of 1939 and went well into 1940, Lolek composed numerous poems and wrote three plays. Each featured a particular Biblical theme and illustrated Lolek's emerging religious mysticism. He also found time to translate Sophocles' *Oedipus Rex* from the Greek into Polish. Lolek wrote his works out first in longhand, and only later transcribed them on a borrowed typewriter. By this time, too, there seemed little doubt in his or anyone else's mind that Lolek's future lay in the theater or the college classroom. But an event that changed Lolek's life was about to take place on a snowy street corner not far from his home.

"A MAGICIAN OF SOULS"

There was nothing special about the tailor shop located at 11 Różana Street, just a few blocks from the Wojtyla apartment. Nor did people know much about its occupant, Jan Tyranowski, a thin, slightly stooped man with a high-pitched voice and greying hair that he combed straight back. For the most part, his neighbors thought him odd; rumor had it that he had once spent time in a mental institution. No one knew whether he had ever been married or what he did when he was not busy making or repairing men's trousers, jackets, and overcoats. What they did not realize was that Tyranowski was the head of a special and very secret religious society: The Living Rosary.

Members of the Living Rosary met not only to recite the rosary, but were also committed to following in their daily lives the Fifteen Mysteries of the rosary. To achieve this goal, Tyranowski needed to find fifteen young men who would pledge to devote themselves to loving God and neighbor every day. The religious character of the group exposed its members to danger from the Nazis, who had already begun to close down seminaries and restrict the activities of the Catholic Church. To create a group of religious activists was even more risky; if the Germans ever found out about the group's existence, the members would be surely sent to the camps where they faced almost certain death.

Tyranowski had often seen Lolek on his way to and from church, and had even gone so far as to observe him at Mass and Bible readings. Then one cold day in February 1940, he approached Lolek at the door of the neighborhood church, asking "May I have a word with you sir?" Mieczys-law Maliński, another young man who was invited to join the society and who, in time, would become Lolek's close friend, recalled his first meeting with Tyranowski, who told him "I have been watching you for some time. You come to mass almost every day. I would like to propose to you that you join the Living Rosary."[17]

Once a week, Lolek and the other young recruits gathered in Tyranowski's second floor room where three sewing machines lay almost buried beneath piles of religious books. Tyranowski, who was called "The Master," met with his charges and suggested readings from theological manuals and books on religion as well as the writings of such Catholic mystics as St. John of the Cross and St. Teresa of Avila. Tyranowski also told the young men to keep a diary so that they could make sure they followed their daily obligations. In their notebooks, next to each subject that was part of the day's routine, there was a blank space. If the young men had fulfilled their daily spiritual requirements, they placed a small cross in the space. The members then read from their diaries when the group reconvened. Lolek also went alone to see Tyranowski, and together they took long walks and talked.

The future pope has always spoken highly of Tyranowski, stating that he was "one of those unknown saints, hidden like a marvelous light at the bottom of life, at a depth where night usually reigns." Because of Tyranowski, Wojtyla believed that he had been given access to a world steeped in spirituality, unlike anything Lolek had ever experienced. As a result of his time with the Living Rosary, Lolek came to understand more fully that in a life stripped of all worldly possessions and devoted to a rigorous program of prayer and meditation, God would fill the emptiness.

The Master's motto was "every moment has to be put to use." Lolek took this view to heart and set about disciplining himself even more in the conduct of daily life. He began with even greater precision to schedule his tasks, from his attending classes in secret to doing his job as a waiter, which he had taken at his uncle's restaurant. He also applied the same rigor to scheduling his religious activities, which by now included attending daily Mass in secret, meeting with the Living Rosary on a weekly basis, reading religious texts, praying, and meditating. One of John Paul II's biographers has suggested that in applying such principles of order and organization, Lolek was extending his father's regimen, which he had put into place after his wife's death. Whatever the inspiration, this amazing sense of discipline, in time, became one of Lolek's most distinctive traits.

THE QUARRY

As busy as Lolek was, he could not ignore what was happening all around him. The Nazis, now in complete control of the general government, began a systematic roundup of all able-bodied Poles to work at forced labor. Anyone without a regular job who was certified by the German authorities ran the risk of being deported to Germany. At twenty years of age and in good health, Lolek was an ideal candidate, as were thousands of others. Fortunately, with the help of friends, he found a job working at the "Eastern German Chemical Works," which produced caustic soda, an ingredient necessary to the manufacture of explosives. Not only was the plant located near Kraków, which meant that Lolek could still live at home with his father, it also meant that he was no longer in danger of being deported.

Lolek began work in September of 1940, and for the next four years, he toiled alongside a number of students whom he had known at the university. Because he was young and strong, he was assigned to the quarry, a massive pit, almost a mile wide, with cliffs dropping hundreds of feet down to the quarry floor. One of his first duties was to help lay railroad track and then load stone into railroad cars. Later, he worked as brakeman, helping maintain the railroad cars. Lolek rarely complained about the backbreaking labor, the long hours, or the bitter cold. (On some days, temperatures inside the quarry fell to thirty degrees below zero.) Only when he had to use a pickax, an effort he was unused to, did he complain. In some ways, Lolek seems to have liked his work, and was particularly appreciative of the extra food rations the job provided. Later he remarked that "when you work, the time runs very fast. A man becomes more a man."[18]

Yet, working in the quarry also acquainted Lolek with the dire poverty that ordinary workers experienced as brute facts of life. He also learned that death was never far away. One day, he witnessed a companion die from a rock fragment that pierced his skull. Lolek never forgot the incident. "They lifted up the body," he wrote in his journal. "They filed past it in silence. Exhaustion and a sense of injustice still emanated from it."[19]

It did not take long before the vigor that Lolek first displayed in his work began to disappear. He lost weight and began to feel cold and exhausted almost all the time. One of his friends remembered how Lolek was known as "the student" by his fellow workers. He looked shabby; one day, standing by the stove, the friend noted Lolek's appearance: a hat with a frayed band covered his head, his jacket pockets bulged, and his many-times mended pants were covered with limestone dust and stiff from splashed oil. On his feet were heavy wooden clogs, the sort that peasants wore. He often traded his ration of vodka coupons for extra meat, bacon fat, or even an extra piece of clothing. The relentless grind of the work and the harsh poverty he endured soon displayed themselves in his thinning face and stooped walk. To add to his worries, the general decline of his father's health troubled him. Karol Sr. appeared to be sinking deep into a depression, caring less and less about life.

What little respite there was from work and worry, Lolek found in the theater. By 1941, he and a number of friends had created the Rhapsodic Theater, an avant-garde and experimental group. Their performances consisted of the spoken word only; there were no costumes, no props, and no scenery. They also had no theater to speak of. Instead, the group gave performances in various private homes, with anywhere from 15 to 20 persons in attendance. It was a highly dangerous undertaking; Lolek later wrote it was essential to keep the theatrical get-togethers a secret, otherwise they risked serious punishment from the Nazis, even deportation to the camps. Twice a week, on Wednesdays and Saturdays, the group met for rehearsals, often at Lolek's apartment where they recited their lines by candlelight, as the Nazis regularly cut the power to Polish homes. In an effort to avoid detection by the Gestapo, the group rotated its meeting place as well as the site of performances. The Rhapsodic Theater was performing in dangerous times; its members "walked past posters announcing an ever-increasing list of executions by firing squads."[20]

Many of the plays that the Rhapsodic Theater performed involved themes of social and political injustice and the struggle of the oppressed. In all, the group met for more than one hundred rehearsals, produced seven plays, and gave twenty-two performances, with Lolek appearing in almost all of them. This was no small accomplishment, as the Gestapo were always watching for any potential signs of disobedience and insurrection. Despite the danger, the members of the Rhapsodic Theater were not just looking for something to do. This theatrical activism was one way of resisting the Germans. For Lolek and the others, the troupe's purpose was "to save our culture from the Occupation," and to "restore the nation's soul."[21]

The Rhapsodic Theater was also allied with a much broader resistance movement in Poland, the UNIA, or Union, a cultural underground organization. The UNIA was committed to stopping the Nazis from eradicating Polish culture. Among other activities, UNIA published an underground newspaper and sponsored lectures, as well as supporting other theatrical ventures similar to those of the Rhapsodic Theater. The UNIA, in turn, was linked to the Polish military resistance movement, which sought to disrupt Nazi occupation, subvert the German army, and shield Jews from capture.

As with all his experiences, the time spent at the Rhapsodic Theater had a tremendous influence on Lolek. Not only did he develop his acting skills, which included connecting emotionally with an audience, Lolek learned how to handle himself in public, important abilities that aided him when he entered the priesthood and rose through the hierarchy of the church. Lolek also came to understand how important the spoken word was in conveying not only emotions but thoughts, ideas, and beliefs to an audience. Speech had the potential to alter people's attitudes, sustain their courage, and spur them to action. Hitler and his chief adversary, Winston Churchill, who became the prime minister of Great Britain on May 10, 1940, also realized the power of the spoken word and, like Karol Wojtyla, used it throughout their careers to great effect.

A SAD END

As busy as he was, Lolek still made time for his father. The two were very close; for Lolek, his father was his one remaining family member and also a reminder of the simpler, happier life he had once enjoyed. On occasion, Karol accompanied Lolek to see the Rhapsodic Theater's performances. But shortly after Christmas, 1940, Karol Sr. became quite ill. The doctor who attended him confined him to his bed. It was up to Lolek to make sure the house was tidy and that his father ate and kept up his strength. Every day on his way home from the quarry, Lolek stopped at the house of his co-worker and friend Juliusz Kydryński, where he visited and sometimes had a bite to eat. When he left, he carried a small metal container of food for his father, which Juliusz's mother had given him.

For Lolek, February 18, 1941, began as a ordinary workday. He went to the quarry and, as was his custom, stopped at a friend's house to eat and then pick up his father's meal. Often Juliusz's sister, Maria, went with Lolek to his house to help prepare the meal. Upon entering the apartment, Maria went to the kitchen; Lolek went to his father's bedroom to check on him. There, to his horror, he found that his father had died. He had died alone, while Lolek was at work. In tears, he ran to the local church to find a priest to administer extreme unction, the Catholic last rites for the dead and dying. That night, Lolek remained in his father's room, praying. Even though Juliusz Kydryński sat with him, Lolek later admitted "I never felt so alone."[22]

His father's death was a major turning point in Lolek's life. As Maria Kydryński saw it, "The fact that he was left alone, without parents, was as if his destiny. He was without obligations, without family." Lolek later stated that "At twenty, I had already lost all the people that I loved, God was in a way preparing me for what would happen. My father was the person who explained to me the mystery of God and made me understand."[23] What Lolek at last came to understand was the plan he thought God had for him, and what he was to become. He was not to be an actor or a teacher. He was to become a priest.

NOTES

1. Jonathan Kwitney, *Man of the Century: The Life and Times of Pope John Paul II* (New York: Henry Holt, 1997), p. 50.

2. Ibid.

3. George Weigel, *Witness to Hope: The Biography of John Paul II* (New York: Harper Collins, 1999), p. 40.

4. Kwitney, p. 51.

5. Kwitney, p. 51, Tad Szulc, *Pope John Paul II: The Biography* (New York: Scribner, 1995), p. 96.

6. Weigel, p. 40.

7. Kwitney, p. 52.

8. Ibid.

9. Szulc, p. 91.

10. Carl Bernstein and Marco Politi, *His Holiness: John Paul II and the Hidden History of Our Time* (New York: Doubleday, 1996), p. 47.

11. Kwitney, p. 55.

12. Ibid., p. 56.

13. Ibid.

14. J. H. Hexter, Richard Pipes, and Anthony Mohlo, *Europe Since 1500* (New York: Harper & Row, 1971), p. 1010.

15. H. R. Trevor Roper, *Hitler's Secret Conversations, 1941–1944* (New York: Farrar, Strauss, & Young, 1953), p. 6.

16. John Cornwell, *Hitler's Pope: The Secret History of Pope Pius XII* (New York: Viking, 1999), p. 182.

17. Bernstein and Politi, p. 50.

18. Kwitney, p. 66.

19. Bernstein and Politi, p. 56.

20. Weigel, p. 65.

21. Ibid.

22. Weigel, p. 68.

23. Kwitney, p. 70.

Chapter 4

THE SECRET SEMINARIAN

After his father's death, Lolek gave up the gloomy apartment in which they had been living and moved in with the Kydryńskis. Although this arrangement provided him with a sense of family, it did not allay his grief. When he was not working, Lolek spent much of his time in his room, praying. Lolek now incorporated another ritual into his daily life. Besides attending morning Mass every day in secret, he also made a point of stopping by the cemetery to visit his father's grave. Friends worried about his mental state, but Lolek seemed to be carrying on with life. He continued to work at the quarry and still participated in the theater. In addition, he was teaching himself French.

By this time, Lolek had been transferred to another job at the quarry. His new manager, a German named Krauze, had grown up among Poles and was apparently sympathetic to their plight, or perhaps he merely respected the life of the mind and all those who cultivated it, whatever their nationality. There was little Krauze could do to help the Poles. But to ease the hardship of the students who worked under his supervision, he found them jobs that were less physically demanding. That way, he reasoned, they might have a little energy left at the end of the day to devote to their studies. Lolek was among those to benefit from Krauze's generosity. His new job was to assist the foreman in placing quarry explosives, which was dangerous work but not physically taxing. Lolek was responsible for setting the charges and attaching fuses inside the holes that other workers had drilled into the limestone.

One of the advantages to the new job was that Lolek no longer spent hours outside in the cold. Instead, he spent most of his day inside the foreman's shack where he could read. Relieved of caring for his father, Lolek now often worked double shifts. The night shifts were quieter, and thus afforded him greater opportunities to read and pray.

Yet, apart from the obvious dangers that came from handling explosives, there were also hidden dangers to Lolek's new job. The foreman warned Lolek more than once that if even a gram of explosives could not be accounted for, he might be hauled off to jail or sent to the camps. The Germans kept careful account of all explosives to make sure that none were stolen to assist the Polish underground. Unknown to Lolek, though, his friend Wojciech Zukrowski, who worked as a miner, was an active member of the Polish resistance, and had on occasion smuggled explosives out of the compound to aid those fighting against the Nazis. Zukrowski never told his friend, not wanting to put Lolek in danger.

By early 1941, it seemed to Lolek that the signs were directing him toward the priesthood. Even though he and his father never talked about Lolek becoming a priest, his father's strict adherence to the Catholic faith had a profound influence on Lolek's outlook. In addition, the continued presence of Father Figlewicz, and the seemingly random encounters he had with people, such as the head foreman, an old man named Labuś at the quarry also influenced Lolek's thinking. "I thought it would be best if he went off to become a priest," Labuś said. "I told him once, 'You better be a priest,' and he just smiled."[1] Taken together, these events and developments proved impossible to ignore.

It was, however, Lolek's involvement with Jan Tyranowski and the Living Rosary that appears finally to have influenced him to enter the priesthood. Years later, as pope, he credited Tyranowski as one of the most inspiring spiritual figures of his early life. While stopping short of giving full credit to Tyranowski for his decision, the pope made it clear that his mentor's influence played a great part in his eventual decision to enter the priesthood.

Still, Lolek wrestled with his decision. It was another year and a half before he decided what to do. In the Roman Catholic Church, entering the priesthood is not considered a career but a calling, a vocation. Those who enter the priesthood respond to an "invitation from God to put on

Jesus Christ" for the rest of their lives.[2] Even though teachers and friends both in Wadowice and Kraków had told Lolek that he was destined for the priesthood, he had disregarded, even resisted, their advice. But he could not ignore God.

In looking back at his life, Lolek concluded that there had been no co-incidences, but rather a series of events that had propelled him to this moment. His sharp intellect, a devout faith, the ability to endure hardship, and even the passion for language, theater, and literature, all seemed to point him not toward a life as an actor or a scholar, but as a priest. Throughout the spring and summer of 1942, Lolek continued to grapple with his decision, and finally became convinced that God had, in fact, selected him. There was only one answer he could give.

A LIFE-CHANGING WALK

In the autumn of 1942, Lolek took a walk. His destination was the old seventeenth-century residence of the archbishop of Kraków, Adam Sapieha, who had addressed Lolek's graduating class a few years earlier. The walk was a short one and did not take Lolek long, but it transported him, literally and figuratively, into another world. After crossing the Old Town market square, Lolek found himself at the address Franciszkańska 3, the tall, stone dwelling that has been the home of the archbishops of Kraków for hundreds of years. After being received at the door, Lolek told the archbishop, "I want to become a priest."[3]

By this time, it had become increasingly dangerous to be a member of any kind of religious order. The Nazis tried in a number of ways to control the Catholic Church, often resorting to coercion, intimidation, and force. They stored weapons in churches. They carted priests and nuns off to the camps. The Gestapo downgraded the seminary to nothing more than a trade school, permitting students to receive no instruction from university professors, and to persuade young men to break off their study for the priesthood. In addition, the Gestapo banned new seminary students, such as Lolek, from attending school, stating that only students enrolled prior to the occupation in 1939 were allowed to finish. In both cases, Archbishop Sapieha instructed his priests to ignore Nazi directives, and instead created a number of diversionary tactics designed to protect young seminarians and their teachers.

The archbishop was determined to keep the seminaries operating just as they had before the war. To accommodate new students, the archbishop hired "parish secretaries" whom he assigned to parishes throughout the archdiocese. The secret mission of these "parish secretaries" was to teach new seminarians, such as Lolek. This arrangement did not, of course, remove the threat of raids by the Gestapo. On one occasion, five students were arrested and were either shot by a firing squad or sent to Auschwitz.

Not wishing to risk the lives of any more students or teachers, Archbishop Sapieha decided to take the seminary entirely underground. Under this system, everything was cloaked under the veil of secrecy, from the students' acceptance into the school to their taking of classes, and even their studying. No one, not even the students' family and friends, could know they had entered the seminary. Such a revelation would put the entire program at risk, to say nothing of the lives of all involved. It was a daring plan that required commitment, fortitude, and courage. For his part, the archbishop was determined to outwit the Gestapo without appearing to do so.

Among the first ten students accepted into the secret Kraków seminary in October 1942, was Karol Wojtyla. Upon entering, he found himself within a carefully organized system that fostered his education while keeping him safe from detection. Each student was assigned to a teacher who supervised his studies. Classes could be held anywhere: in the park, at a private home, in a church, even on a walk, anything to escape or deceive the watchful eye of the Gestapo. All students were encouraged to maintain their jobs, if they had them, and to go about their daily business as if nothing had changed. For Lolek, this meant continuing his job at the quarry, while trying to squeeze in his studies, and still on occasion performing with the Rhapsodic Theater. It made for a very hectic and dangerous life.

Lolek's faith and his enthusiasm for his studies did not cloud the reality of life under the Nazis. Reminders of the power and brutality of the Gestapo were everywhere, but sometimes they touched Lolek in a deeply personal way. By the time he entered the seminary in 1942, the secret police had already arrested several friends and acquaintances. Although some were released, others went to the camps or met their deaths before a firing squad. As if the ordeal of his friends were not enough, Lolek suffered insults because of his faith. Some of his co-workers taunted him, calling him the "little priest" and pelting him with rotten food while he prayed. Lolek took the abuse in stride, and continued to apply himself to his studies. It was also during this period that Lolek discovered the basis for his world view. Reading *Metaphysics*, a book by the Polish philosopher Kazimierz, Lolek confronted the author's contention that the world was ultimately intelligible and rational. Despite the horrors he had witnessed and the hardship and loss he had endured, Lolek accepted the argument. He now discovered, as he later wrote, "a new world of existence...the discovery of the deep reasons for what until then I had only lived and felt.... What intuition and sensibility had until then taught me about the world found solid confirmation."[4] The world not only made sense, but as God's creation it was good, and no evil, however powerful, could triumph over that goodness. It was a profound insight for the young seminarian.

THE SEMINARIAN AND THE ARCHBISHOP

Once again, at a critical juncture in his life, Lolek found a mentor to instruct him. Besides his father, Lolek had long relied on the guidance of Father Figlewicz, his drama teacher Mieczyslaw Kotlarczyk, and Jan Tyranowski. Now, during the autumn of 1942, another figure emerged: Adam Sapieha, the archbishop of Kraków. Descended from the Polish aristocracy, Sapieha's father and grandfather had fought against the tsar. He was, as one historian wrote, "a patrician, a patriot, and a politician."[5] All of these qualities stood him in good stead when dealing with the Nazi occupation of Poland.

Unlike other high-ranking Polish prelates, Sapieha stayed in Kraków instead of fleeing the country when the Germans invaded. His presence comforted and heartened the residents, while creating a series of problems for the Nazis. Sapieha made a point of being seen often in public, and more importantly, of using his authority to work against the Gestapo. The Nazis could have disposed of him, as they did other prominent men and women, but Sapieha was careful not to give them a reason to do so. He rarely confronted the Nazis in a way that would embarrass them, even when lodging protests, complaints, and criticisms. Instead, Sapieha appeared at times to acquiesce, however reluctantly, in the presence of Nazi power, while working quietly behind the scenes to undermine it.

In addition to creating and overseeing the underground seminary, Sapieha aided the Polish resistance movement and provided invaluable information to the Polish government that was in exile in London. He also hid many Jews, helping them to escape the camps by issuing false baptismal certificates that indicated they were Catholics. On occasion, Sapieha even sheltered those who escaped Nazi jails and concentration camps. The murder of five of his close relatives by the Nazis only strengthened Sapieha's resolve. He would never submit, and he vowed he would live to see Poland free of the Nazi scourge. His bravery, resolve, and faith impressed Lolek, giving him the will to fight on.

As Lolek juggled his studies and his job, he also continued his participation in the Rhapsodic Theater, starring in a number of productions during 1942 and 1943. It was becoming evident to Lolek's friends, however, that his mind was occupied elsewhere. Lolek had decided that he wanted to enter the Carmelite monastery after completing his seminary studies, and live the quiet, contemplative life of a monk. Finally in spring of 1943, Lolek made a hard decision. Meeting with Mieczyslaw Kotlarczyk, his old drama teacher who had moved to Kraków the year before, Lolek told him: "Please don't cast me anymore. I'm going to be a priest."[6]

Lolek's decision to enter the priesthood had been met with some dismay among his friends, but Kotlarczyk found it especially difficult to accept. Kotlarczyk believed that Lolek's true destiny was in the theater, not the seminary or the monastery. As one former member of the group stated, "Kotlarczyk was a theater fanatic. He believed that the theater was the most important thing in the world. He said one's duty to God and country could best be fulfilled through the theater."[7] For days he tried to talk Lolek out of his decision, but he failed. Lolek believed that God had chosen him, and that he could not and would not refuse the call. He explained:

> I felt that I cannot be other, cannot realize myself and my mission in life, only as being [a] priest.... It was the time of the war, the great suffering of the whole people. It may be that influenced [my decision].... The direct examples of the priests I met—I'm very grateful to all of them.... But the acting person in this process is the Holy Spirit.[8]

As for the Rhapsodic Theater group, Lolek's news "was some kind of shock...even though he was very religious and didn't try to hide it," said one old friend.[9]

Many of the pope's biographers believe that if the Second World War had not come, then Lolek Wojtyla might very well have gone on to a career in the theater or in the university. Even the pope himself has acknowledged that the advent of the war influenced his decision to become a priest. But by 1943, it was clear that to continue acting was futile; his acting career, like that of so many others, was suffocating due to the occupation. Lolek knew that he could continue his university studies, but to what end? There was no certainty that the Nazis would be defeated and the hope of a free Poland was slowly dying. For Lolek, the decision to enter the priesthood, while not made lightly, and certainly not with false conviction, seemed the most logical and most desirable choice.

By the beginning of 1944 then, Lolek was concentrating exclusively on his seminary studies, while still working at the quarry. Although he kept up his routine, as Archbishop Sapieha insisted, life was still risky. On February 29, 1944, Lolek had another close call with death. While walking home that night, a speeding German army truck hit Lolek from behind. The truck never stopped and vanished into the darkness. Sometime later, Jozefa Florek, who lived nearby, came upon Lolek's body covered with blood. Florek flagged down a passing car, which happened to belong to a German officer. Looking at the comatose Lolek, the officer stopped a truck and ordered the driver to take Lolek to the hospital.

Lolek awoke in the hospital, suffering from a severe concussion, an injured shoulder, and numerous cuts and bruises. For three weeks he lay there, before being taken to a friend's home to recuperate. Lolek later called this experience "a spiritual retreat sent from God."[10] During his convalescence, he prayed, read, and meditated. Any doubts he may have had about his decision to become a priest now evaporated. Despite his terrible experience and his painful injuries, Lolek was now at peace with himself and the decision that he had made.

LIBERATION AND ORDINATION

By the summer of 1944, Kraków was stirring. On June 6, combined Allied forces had landed in Normandy in northern France and were pushing their way toward Berlin, the heart of the Third Reich. Not only did the Germans have the Allied invasion force to contend with, but their effort to destroy their former ally, the Soviet Union, had turned disastrous. Operation Barbarossa, the Nazi code name for the invasion of Russia, had begun on June 22, 1941. The destruction of communism and the conquest and colonization of Russia were cardinal elements of the Nazi plan to dominate Europe. Hitler had made his peace with the Soviets in the weeks before his invasion of Poland, only to postpone the confrontation with Russia until a more opportune moment.

Hitler had originally ordered his generals to plan the invasion for May 15, 1941, but was forced to delay the assault for more than a month until he subdued Yugoslavia and Greece. When at last the Nazis launched their invasion along a broad front, they encountered minimal resistance and inflicted heavy casualties. Between the end of June and the end of September in 1941, the Red Army suffered 2.5 million killed, wounded, or captured. There were, however, some disquieting signs for the invaders.

Russian soldiers and civilians, who had a proven capacity to deal with hardship, fought with incredible determination and courage. After recovering from his initial shock at Hitler's audacity and betrayal, Josef Stalin, the leader of the Soviet Union, never considered surrender. Meanwhile, the German army, far from its bases of supply, began to run short of fuel. To complicate matters, the drivers of supply trucks had to contend with primitive roads that turned into seas of mud when the autumn rains came.

Bitterly cold weather, which arrived early in the winter of 1941, also hampered German efforts. Equipped only with summer uniforms, tens of thousands of German soldiers suffered severe frostbite. Without antifreeze, guns did not fire and engines did not start. Despite these impediments, the German army advanced to within twenty miles of Moscow before a savage Russian counterattack forced German commanders to postpone the final assault. The Russians also denied the Germans Leningrad. During this epic siege, which lasted for two and a half years, the citizens of Leningrad displayed extraordinary resolve in the face of famine, disease, and bombardment, that cost nearly one million lives.

By the end of 1941, the German army had conquered vast Russian territories, but had failed to bring the Russian people to their knees. The Russian campaign demonstrated to the world that the Nazis were not invincible. The turning point came at Stalingrad, an industrial city located along the Volga River.

The battle for Stalingrad was another epic struggle. So brutal was the fighting that at night, when the battle ebbed, the dogs of Stalingrad tried to escape the city by swimming the icy river. Short of food, medicine, weapons, and ammunition, the German commander, General Friedrich Paulus, urged Hitler to order a retreat. He refused, but the German situation was hopeless. On February 2, 1943, the remnants of the German Sixth Army surrendered. In the late spring and early summer of 1944, Russian troops moved through Poland from the east, "liberating" occupied German territory. By July of 1944, the Russians were on the outskirts of Warsaw. On August 1, Polish Home Army General Bor-Komorovski, with a force of between thirty-five and fifty thousand partisans, attacked the German army in Warsaw. Joined in the fight by the city's Polish population, the partisans took control of most of the city by August 4. However, the Germans sent reinforcements that included S.S. police units, a brigade of Russian ex-prisoners, and a brigade of ex-convicts, all of whom had been removed from the war front because of their excessive brutality. Pursued by their enemies, the Polish forces became fragmented and isolated. Forced into the city's refuges—burned out buildings and sewers—the Poles were brutally slaughtered by the Germans. Hearing the news, the people of Kraków waited anxiously to see what would happen next.

On August 6, 1944, a day that in Kraków would become known as "Black Sunday," Mieczyslaw Maliński, a friend of Lolek's who had also decided to become a priest, was leading a group of schoolboys to the outskirts of the city to a field where they played soccer. Maliński was also waiting for Lolek, who had promised to help him on the outing. When Lolek did not appear, Maliński was not concerned. No doubt his friend was either studying or had found something else to do.

Early in the evening, Maliński and his charges returned to the city and spotted groups of German soldiers searching houses, meticulously covering every block. Maliński quickly led the boys away, and soon met up with a number of other men and boys who were fleeing the Germans. As punishment for the Warsaw Uprising, and in an effort to prevent a similar occurrence in Kraków, the Germans were rounding up every male. Even if they held an approved work certificate, the Germans were taking them. Maliński needed to get the boys to safety as fast as possible.

He found temporary shelter in a friend's shed, where they all spent the night. The following morning, he and the boys tried to blend in with the early morning bustle, but it was clear something had happened. The streets were unusually quiet and there were few people about.

In the meantime, Lolek had gone into hiding. When the Germans came to his uncle's house, they searched only the top floors, believing no one was living in the basement. Lolek had spent all of Sunday hiding behind the front door of the basement apartment, "lying face-down . . . in a cross shape." He later told a friend that "he survived by some miracle."[11]

When he heard a soft knock at the door, and decided it could not be the Germans, he peeked out and saw a priest sent by the archbishop to fetch him. Telling Lolek to gather only his essential belongings, the priest escorted him to the archbishop's residence. Irena Szkocka, a neighbor of whom Lolek was quite fond, offered to walk ahead of them to alert them in case there were German soldiers about.

Cautiously, Lolek set out, and soon he was once more at the archbishop's residence, where he was given a priest's cassock and a false identity card. Later that day, he saw his friend Maliński, and learned from him that a mutual friend had been shot and killed during the sweep. By the end of the day, all the seminary students had been located and were in the safety of the archbishop's care. Watching the German sentries marching up and down the street outside his residence, the archbishop remarked, "I prefer not to think what would happen if they ever decided to come here."[12]

Archbishop Sapieha knew that the decision to hide his students at his residence was perilous, but it was the only way he could protect them. Although they understood the importance of such secrecy, it bothered them that they could not do more to aid the war effort. For Lolek, this was doubly the case. It was not in his nature to sit idly by while others put themselves at risk. The archbishop, though, soon learned that Lolek was perhaps in greater danger than the others, because the Nazis were looking for him because he had failed to report to his job at the quarry. With the cooperation of the manager at the quarry, the archbishop arranged to have Lolek's name removed from the worker's roll, and the Nazis discontinued their search.

For the next year, Lolek studied and lived at the archbishop's residence. Everyday, he rose at six and joined his fellow seminarians for a half hour of prayer. Then they attended Mass, where Lolek often assisted the archbishop. Afterward, it was time to study. The archbishop oversaw every aspect of the students' lives, from their studies to their recreation in the courtyard. Lolek responded well to the regimen. He was always reading, and would often hide in the chapel to study so that no one would disturb him. It became clear to the other students that, of all of them, Lolek was the most serious and the most intelligent. Maliński remembered that during discussions, "it was always Wojtyla who ended up being the leader. He was the soul of our little circle."[13]

Compared to his classmates, Lolek lived as if he were already a monk. He often studied on his knees, and received permission to shave his head, cutting away the long hair that had marked him as a flamboyant actor. His clothing consisted of nothing more than a pair of denim pants, an old shirt, and wood clogs, often worn without socks, even in winter. One classmate gave Lolek a warm sweater, which he, in turn, ended up giving away to a poor man. On occasion, his days were brightened by a visit from Jan Tyranowski. Lolek had not completely given up the theater either; sometimes he gave recitations to his classmates, and one day one of the actors from the Rhapsodic Theater even came to the residence to talk about public speaking. He also continued to write poetry, some of which became the foundation for his first published work.

While everyone kept busy during the day, the nights were harder to bear. Everyone's sleep was constantly interrupted by the sounds of falling bombs, air raid sirens, and sporadic gunfire. The Germans were preparing to flee Kraków, but not without leaving behind a wasteland of brick, stone, and concrete. It was common during the day to gaze out the windows of the archbishop's residence and see German soldiers mining the bridges, buildings, and monuments, or carting off wagons and trucks filled with valuables pilfered from homes, museums, and churches. The students knew that it was only a matter of time before the Germans abandoned the city. What would take their place was the question on everyone's lips.

Finally, on January 17, 1945, gunfire echoed outside the residence. Inside, the students were in class and they quickly rushed to the windows. A sudden explosion rattled the windows of the archbishop's residence; smoke was rising in the vicinity of the railroad bridge near the Vistula River to the east of the city. The Germans were pulling out. As the students and the archbishop gathered in the chapel to say Mass, another blast rocked the building, breaking the windows that were still intact. Archbishop Sapieha ordered everyone downstairs to a makeshift bomb shelter where they spent the rest of the night singing hymns, praying, and listening to the sounds of the battle raging outside. The next morning when they ventured upstairs, they saw soldiers wearing different uniforms patrolling the streets. The Soviets had come to Kraków. The Second World War was ending.

With the departure of the Nazis, the seminarians no longer needed to conceal their activities. Instead, Lolek and the seven remaining students spent the next several weeks helping to repair the archbishop's residence and the seminary, which the Germans had used as a prison, and was now without windows or a roof. The Germans though had stolen large portions of the school's library. But the students worked hard and soon not only the residence, but the seminary, its chapel, and courtyard, were repaired, cleaned, and ready for use.

FINALLY IN HIS PLACE

By March 1945, Jagiellonian University had reopened. Students and their teachers, once forced to meet in secret, now came together in the classroom and attempted to ease back into the routine of academic life. But many students, including the few of the seminary students, found themselves taking double course loads to make up for the time lost during the war. Lolek's friend Maliński recalled that many students "dressed in rags, half-starved, and lived in cellars or hovels. Many were ill, especially those who had come from POW or labor camps, not to speak of escapees from extermination camps. But they kept studying."[14] Lolek, too, plunged back into his studies, but still managed to find time to serve as the elected vice president of the student body, as well as to help organize the distribution of used clothing and food to those in need. Beginning in April

1945, Lolek was appointed a teaching assistant, which enabled him to earn money for the first time in months. He now concentrated on studying the works of St. John of the Cross, a famous Spanish mystic, and learning Spanish so that he could read the saint's writings in their original language.

Although life slowly returned to normal, things were different in Kraków and throughout Poland. The Nazis had been vanquished, but the Communists had already begun taking their place. The war and the German occupation had, ironically, destroyed the anti-Communist movement in Poland, since the Soviets were allies against the Nazis during the conflict. It became, for many Poles, unpatriotic to be anti-Communist.

The Yalta Conference between Allied leaders Franklin Delano Roosevelt, Josef Stalin, and Winston Churchill, held in February of 1945, further cemented Communist control of Poland. In effect, the creation of a coalition government in Poland determined that the Communists would dominate policy. Although some believed that a Communist Poland would ensure a more fair economic, political, and legal system, others, Lolek among them, were not convinced. In a letter written in 1941, Lolek was already warning against the unrealistic utopia promised by communism, and that the only thing Polish Communists had in common with Poland was the language. His sentiments in 1945 remain unknown, though it is probable, given his subsequent attitudes and actions, that he, like the Archbishop Sapieha, was cautiously opposed to the new Communist regime.

Adding to tensions within the Polish Catholic hierarchy were its own troubling relations with the Vatican. Under the direction of Pope Pius XII, the Holy See urged the total rejection of, and opposition to, communism. The leaders of the Polish Church, however, who had to deal directly with the new Communist government, took a more prudent and diplomatic approach, even as the new government was working to limit the influence of the Church throughout Poland.

Yet, Archbishop Sapieha was concerned about the new government. He had little use for the Communists; they were, in his mind, not much better than the Nazis. The Catholic Church in Poland was one of the few stable institutions left in the aftermath of the war, and Sapieha believed that the Church had to do more than just look after the spiritual welfare of the faithful.

Taking advantage of the temporary lifting of censorship, the shrewd archbishop instituted a new newspaper, the *Tygodnik Powszechny*, the "Universal Weekly." Reporters and writers for the paper covered current cultural, social, and religious events, but skirted political issues, knowing that if they addressed them openly and directly, the Communists would force them to suspend publication. The "Universal Weekly" quickly earned a reputation as one of the few instruments in which Poles could find reliable information. The newspaper, in fact, was among the few to weather Communist rule in Poland, and is still in operation today. Lolek watched all these events carefully, paying particular attention to the archbishop's political maneuvers. In the process, he learned to deal more realistically and effectively with diplomats and politicians, even when he occupied the weaker position.

Even as Poland's political future was unfolding, Lolek was in the process of completing his last year of study. In 1946, he took his final exams, passing with an "Excellent" in nineteen subjects, a "Very Good" in six, and a "Good" in one. His studies now finished, Lolek decided to apply for admission to the Carmelite monastery in Czerna. To do so, he needed the archbishop's permission. To his surprise and dismay, the archbishop flatly refused his request, telling the order's representative, "I have given permission a hundred times for all kinds of candidates who wanted to join the monastery. I denied it only twice. Once I turned down Father Koslowski who is also from Wadowice. This is the second time I'm going to say no." Sapieha went on to explain to the order's emissary that "with the war over we have only a few priests, and Wojtyla is badly needed in the diocese." He then added prophetically, "and later he will be needed by the whole Church."[15]

So it came to pass that on November 1, 1946, at the Feast of All Saints, Archbishop Sapieha personally ordained Karol Wojtyla a Roman Catholic priest. It was a revealing moment, for Lolek's ordination was carried out six months ahead of his classmates. The archbishop clearly had plans for his young protégé. On the day following his ordination, Father Karol Wojtyla celebrated his first Mass in the Wawel Cathedral, another event filled with symbolic reminders. Guiding him through the ceremony was his old friend Father Figlewicz, for whom Lolek had once served as altar boy and who had been with him the day the Nazis invaded Poland.

Watching him at the altar were members of the Rhapsodic Theater who had come for the occasion. Many people remarked at how handsome Lolek looked in his black cassock and white collar. His hair, once long and unruly, now lay neatly combed to one side. That day, too, Lolek realized his dream of serving a free Poland, if only for a short time. Not all of Lolek's thoughts were on Poland, though, for he said three silent prayers for the departed souls of his mother, his father, and his brother Edmund.

The following day, November 3, Lolek visited his old neighborhood and said Mass once more. In the audience was another mentor: Jan

Tyranowski. On November 4, Father Karol celebrated Mass again. This time former co-workers from the quarry were there to offer their prayers and blessings, as well as many of his colleagues from the Rhapsodic Theater, who came to see their former colleague speak this time not as an actor, but as a representative of God.

Fecit mihi magna, "He has done great things for me," read the message on the holy cards that Lolek distributed to his friends. This surely summed up his life so far. After traveling to Wadowice where he said Mass and performed his first baptism for the daughter of his childhood friend Halina Królikiewicz, Lolek returned to Kraków where he learned that the archbishop wished to meet with him. Sapieha had just returned from Rome, where he been appointed a cardinal. While there, he had decided that it would be wise to send one of the new and very gifted seminary students to Rome to study. He also realized that it might benefit one of his new young priests to study there as well. Lolek was that man. As a consequence, two weeks later, he departed for Rome. It would prove a momentous journey. When he left for Rome in 1946, Poland was still free. When he returned, Poland was once again occupied by a force that lingered longer than anyone thought possible.

NOTES

1. Tad Szulc, *Pope John Paul II: The Biography* (New York: Scribner, 1995), p. 119.

2. George Weigel, *Witness to Hope: The Biography of John Paul II* (New York: Harper Collins, 1999), p. 68.

3. Carl Bernstein and Marco Politi, *His Holiness: John Paul II and the Hidden History of Our Time* (New York: Doubleday, 1996), p. 62.

4. Weigel, p. 70.

5. Bernstein and Politi, p. 63.

6. Jonathan Kwitney, *Man of the Century: The Life and Times of Pope John Paul II* (New York: Henry Holt, 1997), p. 77.

7. Ibid. p. 78.

8. Ibid., p. 75.

9. Ibid., p. 77.

10. Ibid., p. 80.

11. Ibid., p. 85.

12. Ibid.

13. Ibid., p. 86.

14. Ibid., p. 90.

15. Bernstein and Politi, p. 70.

Chapter 5

AN UP-AND-COMING LEADER

"November went by quickly; it was now time *to leave for Rome*."[1] The emphasis placed on those last four words barely conveyed the excitement that Lolek felt. He boarded the train with great excitement. For the first time he was leaving the borders of his homeland. From the window of the moving train he looked at cities known previously only from geography books. For Lolek, the train trip and the visit to Rome marked the beginning of a remarkable journey.

Archbishop Sapieha's decision to send Father Wojtyla to Rome in December of 1946 was in part an act of benevolence and in part a carefully considered plan. The archbishop's memory of his meeting with Lolek almost a decade before when Lolek was a high school student in Wadowice was evidence of his genius for spotting talent. Sapieha now intended for Lolek to fulfill his priestly office in much more than a routine parish assignment.

For Father Wojtyla, the trip to Rome was a revelation. Left behind was the provincial atmosphere of his homeland, awaiting him was the splendor and pageantry of Rome, the capital of the Roman Catholic world. For the next eighteen months, Lolek received a fascinating education in the workings of the Church, which laid the foundation for his rise to a position of leadership in the Church hierarchy.

Arriving in Rome just before Christmas, Father Wojtyla went to the Belgian College, located at No. 26, Via del Quirnale, not far from Quirnale, the presidential palace. More than a century old, the college was housed in a four-story building and graced by a beautiful garden. The building and grounds were hidden behind a large wall and surrounded by trees.

The archbishop's decision to send Lolek to the Belgian College was an unusual move in some ways. Most Polish theological students lived at the Polish College on Piazza Remuria, south of Rome. But space at the college was restricted to those attending the Jesuits' Gregorian University. Archbishop Sapieha was of a more conservative bent than the Jesuits, and had little use for their liberal theology. The Jesuits, though respected for their learning, were also mistrusted for their often controversial and unorthodox views. Instead, he wished for Lolek to study at Angelicum University run by Dominican priests. It was a good match. Lolek was interested in what he believed was the demanding and more traditional theology that the Dominicans taught. The selection of schools was important in another way: it illustrated the growing difference in theology among various priestly orders.

THE BELGIAN COLLEGE

Lolek quickly settled in at the Belgian College. One of twenty-two student-priests, which included Belgians, Italians, and Americans, Lolek took advantage of the opportunity to learn new languages. Already proficient in French, Spanish, and German, he eagerly began learning Italian and English. Mealtimes often found him improving his French with the Belgians and listening intently to the Italians. The Americans, though, aroused Lolek's greatest curiosity. Two Americans studying at the college, Robert Schiefen and Thomas Larkin, took it upon themselves to teach Lolek English. One day as a joke, the two taught Lolek some naughty words. Schiefen later recalled that when they told him what they had done, Lolek laughed and said in English: "Oh, you're pulling my leg!" Schiefen also remembered that Lolek's eagerness to learn was such that at mealtimes, he listened to the American students with an intensity that was "almost like eavesdropping."[2]

Practical joking aside, life at the Belgian College was "pure hardship." In addition to the difficult classes, living conditions at the college were primitive. Indoor plumbing was a recent addition and came only through the courtesy of the British soldiers who had stayed at the college during the liberation of Rome. A year after Lolek arrived, showers were finally installed. As pope, Lolek remembered that the building "was so cold in the winter, that I had a hot-plate under my chair." Summers were oppressive. The students had only the basic necessities in their rooms: a bed, a desk, a chair, and a sink. While Lolek was used to deprivation, he agreed with others on the state of the school's cafeteria: "The food was terrible."[3]

For Lolek, living in Rome offered one exhilarating experience after another. Lolek took full advantage of the opportunity that Archbishop Sapieha had given him. In every spare moment, he visited the great churches, sanctuaries, and museums of Rome. He also traveled extensively throughout Italy, visiting every place and historical site he could. He could not have known that one day he would return to Rome as the head of his church.

SIGNIFICANT ENCOUNTERS

While in Rome, Lolek had two important encounters. The first was a brief audience with Eugenio Pacelli, the aged and ailing Pope Pius XII. The pope had agreed to meet privately with the students of the Belgian College, and although the meeting did not last more than a few minutes, it was memorable because it was rare for young priests to receive an audience with the pope. The meeting with Pius marked Lolek's first visit to the Vatican, and as one biographer suggested, "one can only wonder whether it had occurred to him that one day *he* would be receiving and blessing visitors."[4]

An even more startling encounter awaited Lolek. In March 1947, Lolek, accompanied by Stanislaw Starowieyski, his traveling companion from Kraków, drove to the small town of San Giovanni Rotondo, near Naples. Lolek and Staroweiyski hoped to attend a mass being celebrated by a Capuchin monk, Father Francesco Forgione Pio. Padre Pio had earned a reputation as a miracle worker, and was said sometimes to levitate while celebrating Mass, and to experience the appearance of the stigmata, the wounds that Christ suffered on his hands, feet, and side, during the crucifixion.

Because of Padre Pio's gifts, thousands of devout Catholics traveled to San Giovanni Rotondo to confess their sins and receive the monk's blessing. Legend has it that when Lolek made his confession, Padre Pio knelt at his feet and told Lolek that one day he would wear the Fisherman's ring, the ring of popes. He is also supposed to have predicted that while pope,

Lolek would be the target of an assassin. The story has never been verified, and the pope himself has never commented on it.

Sapieha, now nearing eighty years of age, also came to Rome to visit Lolek in 1947. He brought with him sad news. Jan Tyranowski, the tailor and mentor to Lolek, was dying. Lolek asked permission to return to Kraków to be with him, but was refused. Instead, Sapieha told Lolek to spend the summer traveling through Europe. Accompanied once more by his companion Starowieyski, Lolek went to France, Belgium, and the Netherlands. To help Lolek defray expenses, his American friends donated several hundred dollars.

A SUMMER JOURNEY

Sapieha's order to his protégés was to "study pastoral methods"[5] by visiting as many parishes and talking with as many priests and parishioners as they could. The trip that Lolek took in the summer of 1947 enabled him to appreciate the broader European context. In Paris he came into contact with the worker-priest movement. These experiences, in his first and second years of priesthood, proved enormously important to him. Established by the archbishop of Paris, the worker-priest movement sent priests to the docks and factories where they lived and worked among working-class families. Besides ministering to the Catholic communities and seeking new converts, the priest saw firsthand what life was like among the poor. In this way, the Catholic Church was attempting to understand and meet the material and spiritual needs of men and women in a Europe ravaged by nearly six years of war.

Unlike Starowieyski, who found irksome the rudeness of the French and the overcrowded streets and subways of Paris, Lolek reveled in the noise and humanity. He particularly liked riding the Paris Metro, because it provided him with "an excellent opportunity to practice the internal life," giving himself to meditation while he rode the trains.[6] Starowieyski marveled at his friend's extraordinary devotion and discipline.

Lolek's enthusiasm did not conceal from him a number of troubling sights. "There are saints all over Paris," he wrote to a friend, "but the people are not so religious." Lolek was shocked to find out that only a third of the overwhelming Catholic population of France regularly attended Mass. In Belgium, he found the inhabitants "more or less like the French...a Christianized society...[but] their Catholic religion...lacks the sincere feelings and spontaneity...of our religion."[7]

It was in Belgium, however, that Lolek had perhaps the most important and rewarding experience of the trip when he was placed in charge of the Polish Catholic Mission for the miners in the area around Charleroi, located in the southeastern region of Belgium. Lolek wrote of this assignment that it proved a very fruitful experience. This was his first visit to a coal mine and he was able personally to witness the hard work done by the miners. He also visited the families of Polish immigrants, spoke with them, met the young people and children, and was always shown kindness and warmth. In Charleroi, Lolek found a use for the money somewhat different than the one the American priests who had given it to him intended. Bishop W. Thomas Larkin, then a graduate student in Rome, recalled that Lolek "took the money and went up to the lowlands to minister to Polish refugees. I was kind of impressed that he spent the money that way. He was as poor as a churchmouse."[8]

The summer trip, though exhilarating, was also ultimately a sobering experience for Lolek. Writing many years later of his journey, he noted:

> From different and complementary angles, I was coming to an ever greater appreciation of *Western Europe:* the Europe of the postwar period, a Europe of splendid Gothic cathedrals and yet a Europe threatened by increasing secularization. I understood the challenge that this posed to the Church, and the need to confront this impending danger through new forms of pastoral activity open to a broader participation by the laity.[9]

He returned to Rome at the end of the summer, ready to begin his remaining months of study with renewed vigor and greater determination than ever to revitalize the Church.

A MOST INTERESTING PERSON

Although Lolek was among the quieter and more contemplative students on the campus of Belgian College, he was by no means invisible to his classmates. Monsignor Joseph Lawson, who came to the college in the fall of 1947, remembered always seeing Lolek carrying his prayer book. Lawson recalled how Lolek never used a kneeler when praying, but instead knelt on the hard chapel floor. Another classmate described Lolek as always having a book in hand. Even at the train station "it would come out. He never wasted a minute."[10]

Lolek also spent time with his American classmates, questioning them about life in the United States. He was especially curious about the historic separation of Church and State. "A lot of Europeans didn't buy into religious freedom," said one American classmate. "We told him it worked out very well. The whole idea was new to him."[11]

When not engaged in his studies or carrying out his priestly duties, Lolek kept up his long interest in athletics. He played volleyball or skied in the nearby mountains with friends. Even his most intimate companions noticed, though, that he rarely spoke of himself or his background. Moreover, his growing affection for Italy and its people could not disguise Lolek's homesickness for Poland. He once confided to one friend, "I think about my country all the time."[12] He read the Gospels aloud in Polish every day.

As a final step in his studies, Lolek completed a lengthy dissertation in which he argued that the human intellect was more important than the human will, because the intellect allowed one to begin to understand truth. His ideas showed the influence of early Catholic mystics and thinkers, as well as the influence of Jan Tyranowski. Lolek's research also displayed his marvelous facility with languages. He conducted much of his research in Spanish, discussed ideas with his teachers in Italian, and wrote in Latin. He carried on more informal conversations about his work with friends in French or English. Lolek graduated *magna cum laude* from Belgian College. He had compiled an excellent academic record, though it hardly offered a portent of the future. One of his instructors admitted that in Lolek he "never...saw a sign of a cardinal or a pope." To Cardinal Furstenburg, Director of the College, however, Lolek was the "most outstanding student who ever resided there."[13]

Lolek graduated from Belgian College in 1948. Not until 1978, however, did he receive his degree. Because he could not pay for the publication of his dissertation, which was a requirement for the degree, Lolek did not receive his diploma. Only after he was elected pope did school officials waive this long-standing requirement in order to award Lolek, then Pope John Paul II, his diploma. In June of 1948, with or without a diploma, Lolek was eager to return to his homeland.

Poland had undergone dramatic changes since the end of the Second World War. Perhaps most disturbing was that Poland was once again under the control of a foreign power. Having defeated the Nazis, Soviet troops now occupied Poland, making it a communist satellite. Like the Nazis though, the new Communist government of Poland had little use for the Catholic Church, and Communist officials had even ordered the systematic roundup of more than seven hundred priests who opposed the regime.

Before leaving Rome, Lolek learned that the Communist government of Poland had barred his companion Starowieyski from returning home.

Starowieyski's exile was a severe setback for Sapieha, who believed that Starowieyski had a promising future as a bishop. The Communists did not object to Lolek's return. Thomas Larkin asked his friend whether he was afraid to go home: "He said yes, he was, but people needed him. He could have easily gotten some appointment in Rome.... But [Lolek] said he felt that he was ordained for his people. He owed it to them to go back and help them in anyway he could."[14] On June 25, 1948, Lolek bid his friends farewell and boarded a train for Poland.

A TROUBLED HOMELAND

Lolek "was skin and bones when he came back from Italy," recalled a seminary classmate. To "fatten him up, Cardinal Sapieha sent him to a country parish." Lolek's first assignment as a parish priest was not a remote town, where many Polish clerics got their start. Instead, Sapieha sent his charge to Niegowić, located in the Kraków diocese, in order to give Lolek the best start he could for his pastoral career. Lolek, though, assumed his pastoral duties at another trying moment in Poland's history.

In 1946, Poland was ravaged by war, many of its cities devastated. There was nevertheless a sense of optimism among the people. The war had ended. The Nazi scourge had been removed. For the first time in more than six years, Poles began to look forward to a brighter future. It was not to be. The Soviet government that replaced the Third Reich was in some ways worse, and at the very least, was poised to be in place for a long time. With the advance of the Red Army into Poland in the closing months of the war, Poles soon found themselves subject to Communist rule. By 1948, the Poles found themselves engaged in a bitter struggle, as Soviet soldiers battled Polish resistance fighters. Communist forces defeated those who favored a democratic Poland. The new government falsely accused thousands of Poles of collaborating with the Nazis and executed them. Not long afterward, the government staged a pogrom in which thousands of Jews were killed or deported to Soviet labor camps.

Although under Communist rule, Poland was unique. However brutal and repressive, the Polish government never resorted to the complete destruction of those who threatened its survival. Nor did the government engage in massive public trials and executions of those deemed enemies of the state, as had occurred in the Soviet Union during the 1930s. Collectivization, or the government-ownership of land, was also not carried out in Poland. Instead, the Communists left most of the peasants alone and permitted land to remain in private hands.

The Communists, of course, had other ways of making their presence and their power felt. By the time Lolek returned to Poland in 1948, the country had become a place "where the dawn knock on the door was still expected, where prisons were full and beatings many, where the secret policeman was still his brother's keeper, and the Great Teacher was neither Christ nor Buddha but the megalomanic son of a Georgian shoemaker [Josef Stalin] through whom millions would die."[15]

"The philosophy department is now mainly Marxist. God doesn't exist," a friend told Lolek upon his return.[16] Officially atheist, the Polish Communist government met its strongest opposition in the Catholic Church. Rather than trying to crush the Church, as other Communist rulers did, Polish Communists forged unique relations with the Catholic hierarchy. Because of the strength of the Church in Poland, the government had to be careful not to alienate Poles by dealing harshly with it, while at the same time trying to monitor and control the clergy. The nature of the relations between Church and State in Poland laid the groundwork for a growing resistance movement within the Church that in time proved instrumental in the overthrow of the Communist regime during the 1980s.

For now, the success of the Catholic resistance movement depended largely on the efforts of one man, Stefan Wyszyński. In 1948, amid deepening political turmoil in Poland, Wyszyński was appointed archbishop of Gniezno and Warsaw, and primate of Poland. The task facing him was daunting. But Wyszyński was a patriot who believed that the Church must use its power, influence, and resources to maintain Polish national identity. To accomplish that goal, the clergy not only needed the support of the people, but the people also needed the support of the clergy. The Polish Church had to become the Church of the Common People. As one Polish historian explained, Wyszyński

> set out to change the Polish Church, to make it a Church of the peasants, the common people. He slept little. He worked hard. He visited seminaries and tried to promote priests from peasant circles. He tried to work for social change. And he achieved it. Without this Church of the common people, there could never have been a Solidarity [the Polish labor movement] or a [Lech] Walesa [Solidarity labor leader].[17]

Wyszyński's plan was militant, but carried out peacefully so as not to jeopardize the lives of his priests, nuns, bishops, or people. Although Wyszyński had his critics, who suggested that the Poles might benefit from a more outspoken leader, the archbishop stayed his course. He sensed what the Communists did not: that as the result of their machinations, they had unintentionally created the strongest and most patriotic Catholic Poland in national history. As for Father Karol Wojtyla, observing and working with the Communists was another important chapter in the education of the future pope.

THE COUNTRY PRIEST

On July 28, 1948, Stanislaw Substelny, a parishioner in the church of Niegowić, watched a bedraggled man approach the town on foot. "He wore shabby trousers, a waistcoat, worn-out shoes, and carried a briefcase that I would be ashamed to take with me to the market," Substelny recalled.[18] Initial curiosity at the stranger's identity soon turned to dismay when Substelny learned that the man was the new village priest. After asking for directions to the church from Substelny, the traveler turned to a wayside shrine and knelt down. Praying for a few moments, he picked up his briefcase and made his way to his new home.

To someone who did not know the mind of Cardinal Sapieha, Niegowić appeared to be a desolate outpost. With one of the oldest parishes in the country (the first church had been founded in 1049), Niegowić, home to two hundred souls, was isolated and poor. The current church, built in 1788, was a small wooden structure. Although only thirty miles east of Kraków, Niegowić might as well have been at the end of the earth. At Niegowić, Father Wojtyla was to share pastoral duties with two other priests, Father Kazimierz Ciuba and the pastor, Father Kazimierz Buzała. Sapieha held Buzała in high regard, this being his reason for sending Lolek to him. At the time, Lolek did not realize that many of the most distinguished Polish clergymen had started out working under Father Buzała. Sapieha wanted Lolek to learn from the best.

Living conditions in Niegowić were harsh. There was no electricity or running water, and sanitation left much to be desired. Residents still used kerosene lamps for lighting and the entire village had been recently ravaged by flood. Cows and chickens wandered freely about village streets. Despite conditions, Lolek took on his assignment with characteristic enthusiasm. Whatever reservations the parishioners may have had about the new, young priest, Lolek soon dispelled them with his friendly demeanor and his genuine concern for their welfare.

Lolek quickly settled into a routine: up at 5 A.M. to celebrate Mass. The rest of the day consisted of hearing confessions, performing marriages and baptisms, and administering Extreme Unction, the name given to the sacrament now known as Last Rights, reserved for the gravely ill and the dying. In addition to his priestly duties, Lolek was responsible for providing religious instruction to students in five local schools. If he could not get a ride in the horse-drawn cart of one of the village residents, Lolek made his rounds on foot, regardless of the weather. If fortunate enough to get a ride, Lolek almost always used the time to catch up on his reading. If he had to walk, he prayed. Lolek described a typical day to a friend who once came for a visit:

> You go out in your cassock, your overcoat, your alb [a long white vestment] and biretta [a square silk hat] over the beaten path in the snow. But snow will cling to your cassock, then it will thaw out indoors, and freeze again outside, forming a heavy bell around your legs which gets heavier and heavier, preventing you from taking long strides. By evening you can hardly drag your legs. But you have to go on, because you know that people wait for you, that they wait all year for this meeting.[19]

In Niegowić, Lolek applied some of what he had learned in his encounter with the priest-worker movement in Paris. For instance, Lolek once explained to a friend why it was so important to stay all day in the confessional. For him, one of the most important reasons to hear confession was to be able to establish a dialogue with the person on the other side of the screen. Hearing confession was a serious matter, Lolek explained, and was one of the most important duties a priest had. Without it, or the spiritual bond that results from the sacrament, the priest became little more than an office clerk, faced with solving everyday problems. For Lolek, being available to people and to help them spiritually, while not neglecting their everyday needs, was the most important office a priest could perform. In many cases, Lolek's visits to the homes of the peasants marked the only times that some isolated, rural residents had the opportunity to see a priest. It was becoming clear, too, that Lolek, in his own way, had taken Archbishop Wyszyński's advice. Drawing on what he had learned from the Parisian priests, Lolek worked hard to establish personal relationships with as many of his parishioners as he could.

His dedication and openness made Lolek popular among the villagers. They appreciated that he never looked down on them or regarded them as ignorant. When an old widow had her bedding stolen, Lolek insisted she take his, while he slept on a bare bedstead in the vicarage. He led spirited discussion groups everywhere he went. No space was too small or inconvenient, from the streets to local orchards to the classrooms, for a discussion about the church and its teachings. He helped organize a local theater group, taking a role for himself in its first production. He sang Christmas carols with the parishioners. In memory of Jan Tyranowski, he started a Living Rosary group. He always responded to people's greetings with "So be it!" or "Praise Him!" as a daily way of celebrating the life of Christ. At harvest time, he helped villagers dig ditches, harvest wheat, and separate the chaff, which was done in the old-fashioned way by beating the grain with a flail made of wood and leather.

Lolek had a special gift with children. Mieczyslaw Maliński, an old friend from Kraków who visited Lolek in 1949, was struck by the way the children approached and kissed Lolek's hand. Lolek in return often stroked their heads, sometimes kissing the children's foreheads. Even when the children interrupted him while he was reading, Lolek always made time to talk to them. He helped them with their studies and took them hiking in the woods. With the older children, he organized songfests and discussion groups or played soccer, volleyball, and other games. Stanislaw Wyporek, the son of a local farmer who was employed at the rectory to type Lolek's dissertation, tried to teach Lolek how to ride a bicycle, but met with little success, as Lolek suffered from problems with his balance.

Life in Niegowić appeared simple, orderly, and serene, if busy. But Lolek did not delude himself. He knew there was always the threat of being questioned by Communist authorities. His work among young people was of particular interest to local Communist officials, for it was against the law for priests to work with the young outside of church. Undaunted, Lolek continued his activities, but carefully refrained from becoming too involved in political discussions, much as he had while a student prior to the war. He acknowledged the Communist presence and made the necessary adjustments to it, but he refused to allow the Communists to interfere with his duties or his life.

The secret police tried to disband the parish Young Men's Catholic Association and replace it with a local chapter of the Socialist Youth Group by persuading one youth to inform on Lolek. They failed to find anyone who would betray Father Wojtyla. The police then approached Stanislaw Wyporek who also refused to cooperate with them. They detained him, took him to another village, and severely beat him. The next morning when Lolek found Stanislaw wandering on the road, frightened and in a state of shock, he told him not to worry, that the Communists would eventually finish themselves off. He told Stanislaw that their group had done nothing wrong, and that they should not hesitate to inform the police about their activities. They had nothing to hide. Wyporek recalled many years later that Lolek told them never to resist, but to instead set a good example and practice humility during the hard times.

Wyporek also remembered another incident when he visited Lolek in his apartment in Kraków. Seeing the priest's bookshelves filled with the works of Marx and Engels, Lenin, and Stalin, Stanislaw jokingly asked Lolek if he was converting to another ideology. Lolek replied that in order to understand the enemy, one had to know what the enemy wrote.

One of Lolek's most ambitious undertakings involved the celebration of the fiftieth anniversary of Father Buzała's ordination. Lolek suggested that the best gift would be a new parish church. The parishioners, who had been talking about painting the church fence or cleaning the church grounds, were stunned. How could they afford to build a new church? In the end, though, they agreed to try Lolek's plan. It took almost ten years, but in 1958, the parish at Niegowić had a new brick church. Consecrating the new building was none other than Bishop Karol Wojytla.

Although Lolek relished his duties at Niegowić, Cardinal Sapieha thought the time had come for him to move on. So it was in March of 1949, only nine months after his dusty arrival, that Lolek left the tiny village. He had officiated at thirteen weddings, baptized forty-eight babies, and made countless friends. His next assignment brought him to St. Florian's Church in Kraków, considered one of the better parishes in the city. It was at St. Florian's that Lolek became more deeply engaged in the ongoing struggle between the Polish Communist government and the Roman Catholic Church.

NOTES

1. John Paul II, *Gift and Mystery: On the Fiftieth Anniversary of My Priestly Ordination* (New York: Doubleday, 1996), p. 50.

2. Tad Szulc, *Pope John Paul II: The Biography* (New York: Scribner, 1995), pp. 138–139.

3. Ibid., p. 139.

4. Ibid.

5. Jonathan Kwitney, *Man of the Century: The Life and Times of Pope John Paul II* (New York: Henry Holt, 1997), p. 102.

6. John Paul II, p. 55.

7. Kwitney, p. 102.

8. Ibid.

9. John Paul II., p. 56.

10. Kwitney, p. 102.

11. John Paul II, p. 56.

12. Kwitney, p. 103.

13. Ibid.

14. Ibid., p. 104.

15. Ibid., p. 105.

16. Ibid., p. 109.

17. George Weigel, *Witness to Hope: The Biography of John Paul II* (New York: Harper Collins, 1999), p. 90.

18. Kwitney, p. 109.

19. Ibid., pp. 111–112.

Pope John Paul II, the former Karol Wojtyla, is seen when he was 12, in Wadowice, Poland. (AP/Wide World Photos)

A 1948 photo of Karol Wojtyla, last row, right, during his two-year stay at the Belgian College in Rome. (AP/Wide World Photos)

Karol Cardinal Wojtyla in 1968. (AP/Wide World Photos)

Catholics reach out their hands to touch Pope John Paul II as he proceeds through a waiting crowd of hundreds of thousands of Catholics in Kraków, southern Poland, Sunday, August 18, 2002. Up to four million pilgrims were expected to greet the holy father during his Friday, August 16 to Monday, August 19 homecoming. (AP/Wide World Photos)

Chapter 6

"THE TRAVELING PRIEST"

St. Florian's Church in Kraków is situated five blocks north of Old Town. It is an old parish, dating back to the twelfth century, and is one of the five oldest churches in the city. Because of its proximity to Jagiellonian University, many students attended Mass at St. Florian's. When Father Wojtyla arrived there in 1949, the parish was considered modern, sophisticated, and urban, the complete opposite of Niegowić. The assignment itself was one more piece in Cardinal Sapieha's plan for his young priest.

Lolek arrived at his new assignment in a broken-down horsecart, armed only with a small suitcase and a few books. His parishioners were moved by his show of poverty. Watching him, they wondered what the new priest would be like.

A GOOD FIT

Assigning Lolek to St. Florian's worked to perfection. Although he had enjoyed his time at the parish in Niegowić, St. Florian's was more suited to his scholarly interests, and provided even greater opportunities to work with young people. In addition, the pastor, Father Tadeusz Kurowski, was open to new methods of reaching the congregation and attracting the cultural and intellectual elite of Kraków. Under Father Kurowski's guidance, Lolek was placed in charge of the mission to university students.

Lolek quickly became the most popular priest in the parish, at least among children and young people. While older parishioners complained that his sermons were too long and philosophical, the young ones flocked to hear him. His special rapport with them led to outings and camping trips in the nearby mountains. Not only did these excursions give Lolek an opportunity to be outdoors and to play sports, activities that he cherished, they also provided him with the opportunity to try out some of his ideas in Catholic education. Lolek believed that enjoying nature was another way to honor and grow closer to God.

A typical outing consisted of Lolek celebrating Mass at an altar that he and his companions had built from stones, though sometimes a kayak was used as an altar instead. After Mass, Lolek and the campers hiked in the mountains or kayaked across the lake. Usually Lolek spent most of the day with one boy or girl, listening to them and offering advice. At evening meals, he took turns eating with people from different tents, making sure that he visited with everyone. Young people invariably found him easy to talk to about their most secret fears and hopes.

University students occasionally brought their romantic problems to Lolek, who always spoke frankly to them about their feelings. Unlike other priests, who might be uncomfortable talking about sex, love, and marriage, Lolek believed that candid conversation about these subjects was the best way to guide the young and prevent them from making serious errors in judgment. Instead of simply reciting Catholic doctrine, Lolek spoke from the heart and gave practical as well as spiritual advice, a highly unconventional approach for a Catholic priest of that era, especially in such a place as Poland that was steeped in tradition.

During these outings, Lolek dressed casually, never wearing his cassock or collar. He wanted the young people to feel comfortable and uninhibited with him, not see him only as an authority figure. But in Communist Poland, Father Wojtyla acted as much from political as from personal motives. Not wearing cassock and collar kept him from being recognized as a priest by the police. To aid this deception, he had the students call him *wujek*, which means "uncle" in Polish. Despite these precautions, the police stopped Lolek's entourage on numerous occasions, but were always satisfied that no priest was about.

Lolek worked with the young people, or his "boys and girls"[1] as he affectionately called them, in other ways as well. There were trips to the theater and the movies, and friendly games of chess. He often dropped by students' dorm rooms or apartments to engage in intense discussions about philosophical or theological matters, always remaining careful to avoid talking politics. At St. Florian's, students flocked to hear Lolek's special sermons and lectures on a wide range of topics. His enormous popularity drew record crowds on special holidays or if students knew he was celebrating Mass or conducting a retreat. Lolek also organized a church choir as well as another Living Rosary chapter. Both were overwhelmingly successful. Lolek avoided politics prudently. In this way, he preserved the image he had created of being a "nonpolitical" priest, a tactic that served him well in the years to come.

Avoiding political discussions did not mean that Lolek was uninterested in or unaware of political developments in Poland. As part of his ministry to university students, Lolek gave weekly talks in which, he later wrote, "I would speak . . . about fundamental problems concerning the existence of God and the spiritual nature of the human soul. These were extremely important issues, given the militant atheism being promoted by the Communist regime."[2] Simply by teaching the Catholic faith, Lolek was making a political statement. After he became pope, Lolek maintained strong ties with between fifty and sixty of the students he had counseled at St. Florian's. Some of them eventually came to work for him at the Vatican, either in an official or a private capacity.

During this busy period of his life, Lolek somehow found the time to write a newspaper essay on the worker-priest movement in Paris and also published a selection of his poems. Jerzy Turowicz, one of the editors at the paper, remembers that Lolek "supported the idea of priests' working, which was always very controversial. The problem was that many [priests who worked] became leftists or communists. . . . In most cases, we refuse to publish articles when a priest brings them in, but this one was interesting and well written."[3] Still, Church officials suggested that Lolek publish his work under a pseudonym to avoid difficulties with Communist authorities. He complied.

For the next two and a half years, Lolek continued his work at St. Florian's. He started special classes for couples planning to marry, inviting successful married couples to speak as guest lecturers. Besides his work with young people, he also launched a program aimed at the parents of students to draw them further into the Church. As if he did not have enough to do, Lolek began taking English lessons and dropping by the newly organized Rhapsodic Theater to help out.

A NEW ASSIGNMENT

On July 23, 1951, Lolek's patron, Cardinal Sapieha, died at the age of eighty-five. Thousands of mourners lined the streets of the city as the cardinal's funeral cortege made its way toward Wawel Cathedral. Upon receiving the news of Sapieha's death, Lolek was heartbroken. Little did he realize that the hand of the cardinal continued to shape his destiny, even after death.

Four months after Sapieha's passing, on November 11, 1951, Archbishop Eugeniusz Baziak summoned Father Wojtyla to his residence. Archbishop Baziak told Lolek that now that Sapieha was dead, he was to assume responsibility for him. Ignoring Lolek's look of dismay, Baziak informed him that he was to take a two-year leave of absence from full-time priestly duties in order to study for another doctorate. When Lolek requested permission to continue serving at St. Florian's in addition to studying for another degree, Baziak was quick to rebuke him. But the archbishop relented somewhat, agreeing to allow Lolek to undertake special projects. Baziak also permitted Lolek to celebrate Mass at St. Catherine's Church and maintain contact with his students. Although disappointed, Lolek had no choice but to accept the archbishop's decree.

Because the archbishop had temporarily relieved Lolek of his pastoral duties, he could no longer live at the rectory. Instead, it had been arranged that he would share quarters with Father Ignacy Różæycki, a prominent theologian and professor at Jagiellonian University. While a student, Lolek was free to do as he wished. He worked mainly on his dissertation, but also found time to publish a selection of his poems and begin writing a new play, a three-act drama entitled *Brother of Our God*, which critics and scholars consider the most important literary work that Lolek ever did. The play, advocating Christian revolution in order to correct social ills, predated the similar views of Roman Catholic priests in Latin America known as the "Theology of Liberation." As pope, Lolek had grave misgivings about Liberation Theology, arising from its communist overtones.

During this time, too, Lolek adopted a new look, donning horn-rimmed glasses to correct his nearsightedness. Worsening eyesight did not seem to slow Lolek down when it came to spending time outdoors. His release from parish duties offered him plenty of opportunities to ski, hike, and bike in the nearby Carpathian foothills. His students and colleagues alike were amazed at his stamina. On one camping and hiking trip, Lolek led a sixteen-hour march through the forests and hills, carrying a forty-five pound backpack throughout the entire trek. He hiked long distances, once covering twenty-six miles in a single day. The Kraków Tourism Commission recognized his prowess as a hiker, awarding him a bronze medal for covering 110 miles, including sixty miles in the winter months, over a five-month period. His love of kayaking even led Lolek to enter a competition. His outdoor activities, of course, never kept him from other pursuits. Every Wednesday at 8:15 P.M., Lolek returned to St. Florian's where he met with students to discuss ethics. Whenever possible, he also continued to attend the performances of the Rhapsodic Theater and to write articles for the newspaper *Tygodnik Powszechny.*

Lolek may have initially questioned the archbishop's intentions in removing him from his parish work, but Lolek came to realize that Baziak, like Sapieha, had foreseen his future role in the Church and tried to prepare him for it. In sending Lolek to pursue another doctorate, Baziak not only prepared Father Wojtyla for the future, he also protected him from the growing hostility of Communist authorities in the present.

HARD TIMES

The Communists liked to point to the operation of the Catholic Church in Poland as proof that communism, though atheistic, tolerated religious institutions as long as they did not threaten social and political order. In reality, however, the Communists suffered the Church as long as Catholic officials did as they were told, or appeared to. Under these circumstances, and with the guidance of Bishop Wyszyński, Polish priests learned how to communicate their religious message to the faithful without upsetting the Communists. Wyszyński was famous for issuing subtle challenges to communist propaganda in his lectures and sermons. He used the words *freedom* and *justice,* two terms favored by the Communist regime, to point out the deficiencies of communism. As one biographer of the pope noted, if Wyszyński "wanted to attack a particular aspect of communism, such as disrespect for God, [he] found a similar aspect of capitalist society and attacked that. Poles knew what he meant."[4]

Bishop Wyszyński was no fool; he knew that it was impossible to overthrow the Communist government without endangering the lives of many innocent people and the existence of the Church itself. He and his clergy could quietly and peacefully confront and criticize the Communists on a regular basis. By refusing to give in to Communist demands out of fear or self-interest, the bishop found ways to inspire Poles until the time came when they could strike at the power of the regime with real political force. That sort of resistance though could not yet be undertaken during the 1950s.

In 1953, relations between the Polish Catholic Church and the Communist government took a turn for the worse. With the death of Soviet leader Josef Stalin in March, many thought a reconciliation between Church and State was imminent. Instead, a major controversy erupted in Kraków when the *Tygodnik Powszechny*, which was financed by the Kraków archdiocese, refused to publish Stalin's obituary. In return, Communist authorities shut down the paper and confiscated current issues until the paper's editors acquiesced and agreed to praise Stalin. In addition, because the editorial board refused to fire the editors responsible, the police sealed the offices of the paper. To help the editors who could not publish the paper, Lolek one day stopped by before the police had closed the offices. Instead of offering a poem or an article, which under the circumstances could not have been printed, he withdrew an envelope filled with money from his pocket. It contained half his monthly salary, which he distributed among the editors.

In time, the newspaper found a new home with PAX, a Catholic organization linked to pro-Communist forces. When the government offered to publish the works of priests in a show of tolerance and an attempt to excite popular sympathy for communism, the bishop prohibited any member of the clergy from publishing articles or books without his permission. Lolek, who had already written a number of articles and poems for the paper, made it clear that he would no longer contribute as long as the paper remained under new "management."

Even before the controversy surrounding Stalin's obituary, the Communists in Poland had begun cracking down more forcefully on the Church. Arresting priests was a common occurrence. Those not arrested might have their passports confiscated, preventing them from traveling abroad. In general, the clergy had always to be on guard, for the secret police were everywhere, monitoring activities, conversations, and telephone calls. Priests found themselves placed under constant scrutiny. As they well knew, any act, however innocent, could mean being hauled off for an interrogation session or being thrown in jail. Already one of the most well-known and respected Polish churchmen, Bishop Kaczmarek had been sentenced to a twelve-year prison term on charges of sedition, or disloyalty, toward the government. Wyszyński's arrest and detention just days later was followed shortly by the arrest of another eight bishops and nine hundred priests, sending shockwaves throughout the Catholic community and the nation.

THE TRAVELING PRIEST

Anti-Catholic activities escalated when, in October of 1954, the government closed down the theology department of Jagiellonian University where Lolek had been an instructor of philosophy after completing work on his dissertation. Just like when the Nazis had closed the university more than a decade before, Lolek found himself once more cast into uncertainty. Fortunately, he still had a part-time teaching position at the Catholic University of Lublin, which, unlike Jagiellonian, stated that it was open to all schools of thought, including communism. As a professor of ethics and philosophy, Lolek made for a memorable sight on the campus. Students remembered him sporting a stylish purple beret, horn-rimmed glasses, and a cassock that was frayed from all the time he spent praying on his knees. Lolek's attire was one of the few bright spots on the Lublin campus that year.

Official attitudes toward the Church were becoming increasingly hostile. At Lublin, Communist officials arrested the rector and nine priests who were on the faculty. They also detained and then imprisoned Lolek's new mentor, Archbishop Baziak, as well as the pastor of St. Florian's. Another priest and a layman were arrested and condemned to death for establishing a Living Rosary group for women and a Catholic association for young men. The Communist government was clearly seeking to establish its unquestioned dominance over the Catholic Church in Poland.

To counteract communist oppression, Lolek began meeting secretly with a number of other professors headed by the dean of the faculty of philosophy. At these gatherings, the group discussed their predicament. Rather than giving up and giving in to the Communist government, however, Lolek and the others considered ways to defeat communism spiritually and philosophically. These meetings marked the beginning of Lolek's more outspoken critique of the regime. Whereas he had once kept his opinions to himself, allowing others do the talking about politics, Lolek now articulated his views not only on communism but also on the role of the Church and its clergy in the modern world.

For Lolek, the basic problem with communism was that it distorted the nature of man. The Catholic approach to life, by contrast, was far more realistic in that Catholicism recognized the individuality of man along with the virtues and defects of human nature. Communism tended to view man in more idealistic terms, while believing that the "ideal man," the one created by living in a communist society, would be free of sin and would sacrifice individuality to the collective. For Lolek, the struggle with communism was not one of fighting against it, but one of continuing to preach and live a good Christian life in spite of it. He advised his fellow professors to expand their knowledge and to concentrate on good works instead of wasting time on political issues. Only in this way, Lolek believed, could the Church continue to offer an alternative to the misrepresentations and lies that the Communists disseminated.

POZNA, 1956

Then, on June 28, 1956, a remarkable event took place in Poland. Tens of thousands of workers, demanding pay raises and better living conditions, rioted in the industrial city of Pozna. Marching to Freedom Square in downtown Pozna, the workers sang political songs and religious hymns. Fighting broke out with Communist security forces sent to break up the gathering. Police and soldiers tried to contain the workers by firing into the crowd, but to no avail. The violence continued for three days as Communist authorities rounded up and arrested scores of rioters. By the third day, fifty-four people had been killed and more than two hundred injured. In the wake of the massacre, Poles everywhere vowed never to forget.

The Pozna riots marked a turning point for Poland. In the coming months, tensions mounted between hardliners and more liberal elements in the Polish Communist party. Unlike other Eastern Bloc countries in which Liberal communists were few, Poland had a sizable number who wished to test the rigid government. Challenging Communist authority in Poland, of course, meant challenging the Supreme Soviet in Moscow. For the next several months, Poles watched and waited to see whether a serious confrontation would develop.

In March of 1956, months before the Pozna riots erupted, Boleslaw Bierut, the president of Poland who had been excommunicated for the imprisonment of Cardinal Wyszyński, died. Succeeding him was Edward Ochab, at best a provisional appointment put in office until a more suitable replacement could be found. During this period, moderate Communist leader Wladyslaw Gomulka, who had been under house arrest, stood in the wings, ready to take over leadership of the country. This confusion in the government, in fact, had helped to persuade the workers in Pozna to undertake their uprising. With the government in disarray, workers believed they had a reasonable chance of winning the concessions they sought.

Communist leaders in Moscow would have none of it. Warning Polish government officials to solve their problems with all due haste, the Soviets made it clear that they would not accept a moderate such as Gomulka as president. Soviet Premier Nikita Khrushchev even threatened to intervene on Poland further if the situation was not resolved to their liking. Liberal communists, meanwhile, asked General Waclaw Komar, the commander of the special security forces, if he would be willing to lead his troops against the Soviets, should Khrushchev make good on his threat. Komar agreed.

On October 19, Khrushchev, accompanied by his top military advisors, arrived in Warsaw, where he discovered Gomulka had assumed power. Shouting that Poland was a menace to the whole Soviet bloc. Khrushchev then spent the rest of the day in a closed-door meeting at the Presidential Palace. At the same time, rumors persisted that Soviet troops were advancing on the country. As it turned out, the rumors were true, and the Poles waited anxiously to see how their new president would respond.

Gomulka took a bold stance. He warned that if Khrushchev did not recall Soviet forces, there would be no further talks. Poland, he assured Khrushchev, was quite prepared to go to war. Even as the leaders met, General Komar moved his troops into position to meet the invading Soviets. The clash of Soviet tanks and Polish armored units made Khrushchev thoughtful. Realizing that a war with Poland would bring international condemnation and possible foreign intervention, he agreed to settle the outstanding differences between Poland and the U.S.S.R. through diplomatic channels. At two o'clock in the morning, on October 20, Khrushchev at last formally recognized Gomulka as president and ordered the immediate withdrawal of Soviet troops. The only concession that the Poles made was to let the Soviets maintain their military bases in Poland. The "Polish October," as this sequence of events came to be known, was at an end. It was the first major victory that the Poles had scored against their Soviet adversaries.

A NEW POLAND

With the rise of Gomulka to power, Poland entered a period of liberation not enjoyed by other Soviet-bloc countries. While the country was still under Communist leadership, restrictions eased and Poles made the most of the opportunity that the more liberal regime offered. To earn additional good will, the government released political prisoners and lifted bans imposed upon newspapers and other publications once deemed "subversive." Within six days of his showdown with Khrushchev, Gomulka or-

dered the release of Cardinal Wyszyński. In doing so, Gomulka acknowledged the cardinal's importance in restoring order. More fully than his
predecessors, Gomulka understood that the political and economic stability of Poland depended on a collaborative relationship between the government and the Church.

Wyszyński was pleased to be released from prison, but not so grateful
that he accepted Communist generosity without insisting on conditions
of his own. In return for the aid of the Church in maintaining order,
Wyszyński demanded the immediate release of all imprisoned bishops and
priests, the reinstatement of bishops forced out of their dioceses, and the
repeal of the 1953 decree that authorized the State rather than the Vatican to appoint all bishops. Gomulka agreed to the cardinal's terms, and it
appeared that a new era of cordial relations had begun between the
Church and the government in Poland.

SCHOLAR-PRIEST

Throughout the October crisis, Lolek remained silent, preferring to
concentrate on his classes. Toward the end of 1956, Lolek received some
wonderful news: he had been appointed chairman of the ethics department at Catholic University. The appointment was prestigious, moving
the thirty-six-year-old Lolek into the leadership position of one of the
most respected and important centers of Catholic philosophy and theology in Eastern Europe.

Though the university appointment meant spending more time in
Lublin, Lolek did not cut his ties with Kraków. Instead, he maintained a
brutal commuting schedule, regularly traveling back and forth between
the two cities, a journey of twelve hours. True to form, Lolek made the
most of the trip, either spending his time reading or praying.

For the next eighteen months, Lolek kept up this hectic pace, dividing
his time between teaching classes, performing administrative duties as department head, presenting outside lectures, and writing articles, poems,
and his first book. He also produced what many scholars consider an important essay on Church law, which eventually led to his involvement
with drafting new canon law.

Both inside and outside the classroom, Lolek found admirers. Captivated by his teaching and his personality, students filled his classes to capacity and beyond. They sat on the floor and the windowsills, or stood
along the walls in the back of the room, just for a chance to bask in the
wisdom of the celebrated Father Wojtyla. Again, his personal style caught

the students' attention. Still wearing a frayed cassock, Lolek also donned olive green trousers and large shapeless shoes. Busy as he was, he always made himself available to talk with students, who flocked to him with questions. He had developed a reputation as something of a soft touch, willing to lend small sums of money to students in need, which invariably he told students not to bother repaying. Students also met him for confession, often telling him things they would never divulge to another priest. His ability to listen, coupled with his serious but kind demeanor, soon brought "Uncle" scores of followers among the student body and faculty alike.

Lolek was also known for his sense of humor. One student has sworn that his teacher once slid down a railing in his cassock. Another student remembered that a clerk brought a message to Lolek, who was in the middle of teaching. Embarrassed at having interrupted Lolek's lecture, the clerk knelt before him as he delivered the message. Lolek responded by also kneeling, which elicited peels of laughter from the students.

For all his popularity, Lolek never forgot that he was a priest bound to uphold the teachings of the Catholic Church. Yet even in the most important part of his life, he was unconventional. While holding fast to traditional Catholic doctrine, he stressed to his students and colleagues the necessity of keeping the faith in "all domains of life" and not relying on erudite theological arguments when real lives were at stake and real souls in jeopardy. Lolek, for instance, believed strongly in the Catholic condemnation of abortion, which, to his sorrow, was available on demand in Communist Poland. At the same time, he argued that the Church had an obligation to help women find alternatives to abortion. Merely condemning them as sinners for having terminated their pregnancies constituted a failure of Christian love. Then, too, should a woman facing difficult circumstances decide to have a baby, the Church and the whole Catholic community had a responsibility to help her raise and provide for the child.

BISHOP WOJTYLA

The first part of July 1958, found Lolek traveling with friends and students in the mountains of Poland. At that very moment, however, important events were unfolding thousands of miles away that would change his life forever. In Castel Gandolfo, the summer residence of Pius XII, the pope, aged and ill, was devoting his waning energies to the endless paperwork that the papacy entailed. Among the documents on his desk were nominations for six new suffragans, or auxiliary bishops, in Poland. Because the liberal Communist government allowed the pope to appoint suffragan bishops, though not diocesan bishops or archbishops, Pius was mulling over his options.

One of the posts to be filled was in Kraków. On July 8, 1958, the pope nominated as titular bishop of Ombia, and the auxiliary bishop of Kraków, Father Karol Wojtyla. Although it is unlikely that Pius made the nomination based on his earlier meeting with Lolek, he did take into consideration the recommendations of Polish clerics. The next step was to inform Catholic authorities in Poland of his choice and determine whether it was acceptable to them.

It was. Archbishop Baziak, who had been acting as Lolek's mentor after Cardinal Sapieha's death, formally nominated Father Wojtyla later that summer. His decision to support Lolek's candidacy caught many by surprise. Though well thought of and well liked, Lolek had virtually no administrative and little in the way of pastoral experience outside of his brief postings at Niegowić and St. Florian's. Many also thought that at thirty-eight, Lolek was too young to be named a bishop. Others were less concerned, seeing the appointment as the next step in the plan that Sapieha had devised before his death. Without Baziak's help, though, the nomination would not have gone forward, and chances are slim that Lolek would have become pope. One influential figure in the Polish Catholic Church has said that if Baziak had not picked Wojtyla for bishop, he would have spent the rest of his life as a distinguished professor at Catholic University in Lublin; most certainly he would never have been pope.

In at least one respect, Lolek's nomination was controversial. Baziak himself traveled to Rome to voice his approval of the selection to Pius XII. Standard procedure dictated that bishops made their views known to the pope indirectly, using a cardinal as the intermediary. In this case, the go-between would have been Cardinal Wyszyński. It was no secret that Baziak and Wyszyński were not on good terms. Baziak apparently intended his unprecedented maneuver to circumvent the cardinal and challenge his authority. Through no fault of his own, Lolek found himself in the middle of a power struggle between his superiors.

Back from his mountain vacation, Lolek was in Kraków, busily at work on his book and as yet only dimly unaware of the controversy of which he was the focus. On August 18, 1958, he received a telephone call from an assistant to the primate of Warsaw, summoning him to a meeting with Cardinal Wyszyński. From the caller, Father Wojtyla learned that his appointment as auxiliary bishop had been approved. There is no record of Lolek's reaction to the news, but his students were both overjoyed and saddened. When it came time for Lolek to leave, they carried him to the train station on their shoulders.

On September 28, 1958, Father Karol Wojtyla was ordained a bishop in a ceremony at Wawel Cathedral, with his friend and mentor Archbishop Baziak presiding. The church was filled with men and women who had known Lolek at some time in his life. There were parishioners from the two churches to which he had been assigned. There were members of the theater and Living Rosary groups. There were former students, fellow priests, and long-time colleagues from the university. His old friend from seminary, Father Maliński, recalled that during the ceremony, Lolek appeared tense and reflective, standing with his head down, his face tight and sad-looking. When the ceremony ended, Lolek looked visibly happier, and saluted his friends as he left the cathedral. As bishop, Lolek adopted the Latin motto *Totus tuus*, "All Yours." Since then, the motto has appeared on every piece of correspondence that he has written and every document issued in his name.

Lolek may have been a bishop, but he refused to stop doing the things he enjoyed or to alter his relations with people. Those who knew both Bishop Wojtyla and Cardinal Wyszyński soon began comparing them, much to the cardinal's displeasure. Where people found the cardinal haughty and intimidating, they found Lolek humble and accommodating. Nor did Bishop Wojtyla exchange his sense of humor for a miter and crosier. Arriving at a friend's house wearing his bishop's purple cord around his cassock sleeve, the man's young son asked Lolek: "Oh, have you become a railway worker?"[5] Those employed on the Polish railroad also wore black coats with purple stripes. Obviously amused by the question, Bishop Wojtyla replied that he had in fact gone to work for the railroad, and proceeded to describe the different trains on which he rode. As priest and professor so as bishop, Lolek made himself accessible to people, especially to children. He also continued to write poetry, but wondered aloud to one editor whether a bishop should publish poetry.

According to friends, Lolek asked for three things when he became a bishop. He wanted a separate canoe and tent for his camping trips, a folding desk and reading lamp in the car in which he rode, and the reburial of his mother and brother in Kraków next to his father's grave.

News of Lolek's unconventional conduct and requests soon reached Cardinal Wyszyński. In response, the cardinal made a point of letting everyone know his displeasure with the appointment of Lolek as bishop and his outrage that Baziak had gone to the pope behind his back. Other officials in the Polish Catholic hierarchy were equally unimpressed with

Lolek, complaining that he kept too close company with students. One bishop in particular complained that when swimming, Lolek wore a bathing suit just like the other men. One of Lolek's supporters replied, "You want that they go swimming *without* their slips [bathing suits]?"[6]

Wyszyński and Wojtyla finally met at a conference of Polish church officials. As the cardinal was lecturing, Lolek sat in the back of the room reading. Wyszyński grew more and more irritated at Lolek's apparent inattentiveness. At last he said, "Now Bishop Wojtyla is going to tell us what we are talking about," at which point Lolek looked up from his reading and proceeded to explain the substance of the cardinal's lecture.[7] That Lolek had been paying close attention to Wyszyński's words only further exasperated the cardinal.

Not long after his consecration as bishop, Lolek, along with thousands of other Poles, came to greet the visiting archbishop of Vienna, Franz König, whose train had stopped near the Czech-Polish border. "Everyone was laughing and talking" when the archbishop noticed a "shy young priest." Coming up to the archbishop, the priest introduced himself as the new bishop. König remembered his surprise at learning that the young man "was the new bishop and he had come to greet me." Intrigued, and eager to learn more about Lolek, the archbishop decided to change his plans and spend the night in Kraków. König later remarked that, "If anybody that day would have said to me he would be the pope, I would have said he was crazy."[8] Little did either man realize the future importance of their meeting.

On October 8, 1958, Pope Pius XII died. For the next three days, the College of Cardinals who met to choose the next pope, remained deadlocked through the first three rounds of voting. Finally the cardinals agreed on a candidate: Angelo Guiseppe Roncalli, a seventy-seven-year-old cardinal from Venice. Taking the name John XXIII, Cardinal Roncalli ascended to the papacy on October 28, 1958, one month to the day after Lolek's consecration as bishop. At the instigation of the new pope, Vatican Council II, a movement to reform the church, was summoned. In the first general council of the Church in more than a century, Bishop Wojtyla would play an important role that would move him closer to the papacy.

NOTES

1. Carl Bernstein and Marco Politi, *His Holiness: John Paul II and the Hidden History of Our Time* (New York: Doubleday, 1996), p. 79.

2. John Paul II, *Gift and Mystery: On the Fiftieth Anniversary of My Priestly Ordination* (New York: Doubleday, 1996), p. 64.

3. Jonathan Kwitney, *Man of the Century: The Life and Times of Pope John Paul II* (New York: Henry Holt, 1997), pp. 114–115.

4. Kwitney, p. 126.

5. Ibid., p. 160.

6. Ibid., p. 161.

7. Ibid.

8. Ibid., p. 162.

Chapter 7

THE CARDINAL

Less than three months after his election, Pope John XXIII announced plans for the Second Vatican Council, which he called *Aggiornamento*, or "bringing up to date." The last Vatican Council had been held a century earlier; clearly it was time for the Church to reevaluate its mission for the second half of the twentieth century. The pope sought new ways to address the problems Catholics now faced. One of the pope's goals for the Council was to restore Christian unity by ending differences between the various Christian churches. He also wanted to promote worldwide religious freedom and revitalize the relationship between the Catholic hierarchy, clergy, and faithful.

To get recommendations for the agenda, the Vatican sent more than 2,500 questionnaires to bishops and cardinals throughout the world. These clergy became known as the "Council Fathers," who were scheduled to convene in October, 1962. Bishop Karol Wojtyla received one of these questionnaires. Excited by the prospect of attending a general council of the Church, he was among the first to return his comments and to begin making preparations to travel to Rome.

AN EVIL INFLUENCE

In the meantime, Lolek kept busy attending to his new duties as bishop. He did not slow his frenetic pace. If anything, he added to the various tasks that he performed nearly every day. He now celebrated daily Mass at a number of different churches, in addition to visiting parishes and convents, meeting with clergy, students, and laypeople, and writing articles and poems.

As bishop, he worked in an office located in the archbishop's palace on Franciszkańska Street, which was the center of the Kraków Metropolitan Curia. He had his own living quarters, a welcome relief from years of sharing cramped houses with others. His bishop's apartment even had its own chapel, where Lolek spent numerous hours in prayer and meditation. Helping him to take care of his household was his father's half-sister, Stefania Adeljda Wojtyla.

Although enthusiastic about his new role and responsibilities, Lolek had serious concerns. His life was not without its complications. Within six months of his appointment as bishop, Lolek drew unwelcome attention from Communist authorities. Although he was doing nothing extraordinary—nothing that he had not previously done while serving as a parish priest—his higher profile as a bishop prompted the government to deem him a bad influence on Polish society, and protest his activities.

In March, Wikto Boniecki, Chairman of the Kraków Presidium of the National Council, an organization that acted as a front for the Communist government, sent a two-page letter to Archbishop Baziak charging that Lolek's activities encouraged the clergy to violate the law. The archdiocese was being held responsible for its failure to act against such violations. Examples of the violations Lolek had committed or encouraged included "meditation days" for lawyers, physicians, teachers, and youth. According to Boniecki, organizing such occasions promoted a divisive atmosphere to the so-called socialist unity of Kraków society.

Baziak then turned over the letter to Lolek, who in turn wrote back, denouncing the Council and reminding them that there was no law forbidding Catholic clergy from conducting their pastoral work. Further, the "meditation days" that Boniecki believed were in violation were nothing more than meetings of a religious nature. Lolek went on to point out that the Communist state constitution granted freedom of worship and conscience and accused Boniecki of violating the very laws he was supposed to uphold. Communist officials backed off, but the entire situation made them wary of the new bishop.

The Communist accusations troubled Lolek, but unlike in the past, he now spoke out on political matters he considered to be the inviolability of the rights of the Church and his fellow Poles. Despite the Communist rebuke, Lolek kept busy with his ecclesiastical and educational activities. When at last the hectic schedule proved too much for him and he fell seriously ill with mononucleosis, his doctor ordered him to bed for a complete rest. Afterward, Lolek enjoyed a lengthy convalescence that gave him an opportunity to hike, ski, and kayak. To regain his strength, Lolek also began doing calisthenics in his bedroom, a practice that he continued as pope. Although he recovered from mono, illness plagued him for the next few years, causing him to cancel a number of trips and speaking engagements.

AUTHOR AND PLAYWRIGHT

Slowed by illness, Lolek somehow found the energy to write. He published essays, speeches, and poems, and in 1962, completed a book entitled *Love and Responsibility,* and a play, *In Front of the Jeweler's Shop.* Both works dealt with marriage. Drawing on his own research and experience in counseling engaged and married couples, Lolek addressed the subjects of monogamy, equality, and birth control. In both book and play, Lolek tried to combine Catholic teachings with a practical and realistic vision of marriage. To everyone's surprise, including Lolek's, *Love and Responsibility* became a nationwide bestseller in Poland. Hundreds of thousands of copies were sold, and after Lolek became pope, new editions were published in English, French, Spanish, Italian, German, Swedish, and Japanese.

In Front of the Jeweler's Shop was a three-act play, which Lolek wrote under the pen name Andrzej Jawień, the same name he used to write articles and poems. Instead of dialogue, the characters deliver their lines as monologues, to the accompaniment of a backstage chorus. The play was later translated into Italian and broadcast over the radio. It was also made into a motion picture starring Burt Lancaster.

PROTECTOR OF THE PEOPLE

By the early 1960s, it was becoming clear that the promise of the Polish October had faded as the current Polish government adopted an increasingly hard line. The government appeared now to be more in step with Moscow, and it began phasing out many of the liberal reforms. Once more the government tried to intimidate the Catholic Church and to harass the clergy.

Although not stridently critical of the government, Lolek continued to defend the Church and to insist that Catholics had the right to worship and to participate in church-related activities. He took care not to condemn Catholics who believed in socialism. Instead he displayed an open-mindedness that baffled many, both inside and outside the Church. He ignored government warnings, but also did not go out of his way to provoke authorities as did some of his colleagues. Lolek was also willing to compromise when necessary, but never gave in to the government on matters he considered essential to the integrity and survival of the Church.

Perhaps the most striking example of Lolek's method of dealing with the Communists came in 1962. On June 15, Lolek's patron, Archbishop Baziak, died. The following day, Catholic officials decided that Lolek should serve as capitular vicar, a temporary replacement for the archbishop. Lolek was ready for the challenge and had every intention of using that authority. Two months later, Communist authorities seized the convent of the Sisters of Our Lady of Mercy in Kraków. Lolek soon arrived on the scene and reassured the nuns that everything would be alright. When, a few weeks later, Communist authorities seized another Church-owned property, the downtown buildings of the Kraków Seminary, Lolek immediately ordered his driver to take him to the regional headquarters of the government. There he met with the Communist Secretary Lucjan Motyka. It was the first time ever that a Polish bishop had gone on his own to see Communist leaders.

Lolek's speedy challenge to the takeover of the seminary enabled him to work out a compromise. He agreed to allow the government to establish a state teachers' college on the third floor of the seminary; the Church, however, would continue to occupy the rest of the building with no interference from the Communists. Despite Lolek's negotiating skill, the incident was not over. Two weeks later, Lolek, accompanied by several members of the seminary faculty and a number of students, led a silent march to another building around the corner, which they dedicated to the Blessed Mother, a not-so-subtle reminder to the Communists of which institution really owned the building. From that point on, Communist authorities knew that the acting archbishop of Kraków was a man to be reckoned with.

THE COUNCIL

In 1962, of the 25 Polish bishops who applied for passports to travel to Rome for Vatican II, as the pope's Second Vatican Council was called, only 10 were allowed to go. One of those 10, surprisingly, was the acting archbishop of Kraków, Karol Wojtyla. After 14 years, Lolek was returning to Rome. He had left the city as a novice priest, unsure of direction. He now returned as an acting archbishop, confident, self-assured, and ready to do business.

In October 1962, the 2,381 bishops and cardinals at last met for the commencement of the Second Vatican Council. In all, they represented 141 countries and included cardinals and bishops from Japan and Africa, marking the first time that countries outside the traditional European circle were represented. The Second Vatican Council proved to be a revolution of sorts for the Church. What Pope John had initially envisioned as a meeting of bishops and cardinals lasting for a few months, in fact turned out to be a series of four meetings over the course of three years. When it was over, the Roman Catholic Church had undergone a number of significant reforms that many believed were comparable to the types of changes made by the Church almost four centuries earlier at the Council of Trent in the sixteenth century.

Underlying much of the Council's agenda was the need to implement Church reforms. Among the changes that would eventually be adopted were liturgical reform, the use of vernacular language instead of the traditional Latin in saying Mass, a mending of strained relations between the Church and Protestant and Orthodox denominations, the disavowal of anti-Semitism, and an acknowledgment of the idea of freedom of conscience.

The movement for reform enjoyed its greatest support among the delegations from Western Europe and the United States. But the Polish delegation found itself in a unique position at Vatican II. Poland was the only Eastern European Communist country represented at the Council, and because of Cardinal Wyszyński's own stance against communism, many were interested in hearing his views on the proposed reforms.

Many writers have subsequently exaggerated Lolek's influence at Vatican II; he was at the time a virtual unknown outside of Poland. That did not stop him, however, from offering his views and becoming an active participant in the Council, even if it meant voting against other members of the Polish delegation. During the first session, Lolek delivered two speeches before the Council and submitted two written pieces to the

Council agenda. His thoughtfulness and ability to discuss even the most difficult issues soon earned him the respect of many bishops and cardinals.

Lolek also found time to become reacquainted with Rome and to hike in the hills surrounding the city. He also had a memorable introduction to the American dessert, apple pie á la mode. When first presented with a piece of pie with ice cream on top, he remarked, "What a strange custom. What did you say *that* was?"[1]

Another piece of Church business that wasn't connected with the proceedings of the Council directly concerned Lolek. At the end of the first session in December 1962, Pope John met with Cardinal Wyszyński to discuss a permanent replacement to fill the vacancy left by Archbishop Baziak's death. The cardinal was clearly uncomfortable discussing candidates to replace Baziak, telling the pope that "Kraków will have to wait...because of the general situation."[2] Wyszyński could not easily reject Lolek's candidacy, for he had done a good job since taking over for Baziak. But Wyszyński in no way wished to endorse Lolek or give Pope John the impression that he approved of him becoming archbishop.

PEACE ON EARTH

International affairs overshadowed the first session of the Second Vatican Council. In October of 1962, United States military intelligence learned that the Soviets had deployed nuclear missiles in Cuba, only 90 miles off the coast of Florida. When President John F. Kennedy issued an ultimatum to Soviet Premier Nikita Khrushchev to remove the weapons or risk the outbreak of nuclear war, the pope appealed to both men to consider the dire implications of their actions and to exercise sober judgment. Despite Soviet aggression, Pope John believed that a policy of *Ostpolitik*, or openness, would do more to ease international tensions than an unyielding anti-communism. Although some supported the pope's ideas, most high-ranking Church officials disapproved of his apparent willingness to compromise with the Communists. That soft approach, they believed, would make the Church appear weak and vulnerable. Others feared that the pope's attitude would open the way for the Communists to further their goals by gaining a stronger presence in the governments of Western European nations.

Critics did not sway the pope. To reinforce his views, he issued an encyclical "*Pacem in Terris*," or "Peace on Earth." With this important document, the pope broke with a long-standing tradition of addressing only Catholics. Instead, he spoke "To All Men of Good Will," which in his mind also included some Communists. Outlining his disagreements with communism, the pope nonetheless maintained that "Communism could change and should be worked with."[3] He then chastised the leaders of both the East and the West for violating human rights, particularly those of Third World peoples. Finally, with both sides in the Cold War calling for limits on nuclear weapons testing, the pope called for an outright ban on all such weapons. John XXIII, however, did not live to see the work he had begun brought to completion. He died in June of 1963.

AN UNOCCUPIED SEAT

By the end of December, 1962, Lolek was back in Kraków. Still trying to evaluate the Second Vatican Council, he was becoming increasingly restive with his temporary appointment as capitular vicar. He could do little to alter his situation; his fate was in the hands of Cardinal Wyszyński, who had made his feelings about Lolek clear. Those who knew both men agreed that the cardinal did not wish to see Lolek made archbishop of Kraków.

In order to appoint a new archbishop, the cardinal had to submit a list of at least three names to the government, which, in turn, could accept or reject any or all of the nominees. When the government approved a candidate, the cardinal then sent the nomination to the Vatican where the pope made the final decision. In approving Lolek's candidacy, the Communists unwittingly brought to power the man who, almost two decades later, played a key role in their demise.

By 1963, the cardinal was growing anxious to find a permanent replacement for the late Archbishop Baziak. Noticeably absent from the list of candidates that he compiled was the name of the acting archbishop, Karol Wojtyla. There were a number of reasons to explain Wyszyński's resentment of Lolek and his reluctance to support his rise to archbishop. The first was a generational difference. Born nearly twenty years before Lolek, the cardinal had grown up under the yoke of foreign occupation. The experience of seeing his beloved Poland disappear from the map of Europe, carved up by the Austrians, Germans, and Russians, shaped the cardinal's view of communism. For the cardinal, compromise was the most desirable way to deal with the Communists, if only to avoid more severe reprisals such as an invasion and the loss of Poland as a country. In his defense of the Catholic Church, Lolek, on the contrary, could practice a strategy of both compromise and confrontation, depending on the situation and what was at stake. Based on what had already taken place between Lolek and the Communist authorities, the cardinal was alarmed at the possibility of more direct and overt confrontations.

Second, Wyszyński viewed with suspicion Lolek's position on social questions. Some even suggested that the cardinal was both jealous and frightened of Lolek's progressive stance on many Church issues. His engagement in secular activities such as writing poetry and plays also upset the old man, who thought such activities unseemly for a cleric. As one churchman saw it, however, Wyszyński's resistance to appointing Lolek was far more basic: the primate believed that the people he named to high posts should be mediocrities, something that Wojtyla clearly was not.

During the next year, the cardinal submitted six names to the Communists, each of whom the members of the Department of Religious Denominations subjected to intense scrutiny. Since the government had three months to review every nomination, the cardinal submitted one name at a time. In the end, the committee rejected all six. The cardinal finally put forth Lolek's name, bowing to pressure from other Church officials, many of whom had seen Lolek at Vatican II and had been impressed with his abilities.

To nearly everyone's surprise, the government accepted Lolek's nomination. Misunderstanding the nature of the cardinal's disapproval, the Communist authorities apparently thought that his disfavor made Lolek the perfect candidate. They had either forgotten or overlooked Lolek's previous criticisms of the government, and recalled only the diplomatic way in which he handled the seminary takeover a year earlier. They also believed Lolek to be uninterested in politics and content with the status quo, all of which made him easier to control. The tension between Wyszyński and Lolek, the Communists reasoned, would also divide and weaken the church in Poland. On December 30, 1963, therefore, Karol Wojtyla was named Metropolitan Archbishop of Kraków by the new pope, Paul VI. Three months later, on March 3, 1964, he was formally installed as Archbishop at Wawel Cathedral. He was forty-three years old.

PAUL VI AND THE CONTINUATION OF VATICAN COUNCIL II

The successor of Pope John XXIII was another Italian-born cardinal, Giovanni Battista Montini, who took the name Paul VI. The new pope was as equally committed as his predecessor had been to reforming the church. Paul VI thus renewed the Second Vatican Council and, with his nomination for archbishop pending, Lolek again set out for Rome in the autumn of 1963. During the second session of Vatican II, he gave one speech before the Council in which he discussed modernization of the Church and its liturgy. At the end of the session in December, Lolek made his first journey outside of Europe, traveling with a group of bishops on a 10-day visit to the Holy Land.

The following year, Lolek returned to Rome for the third session of Vatican II. It was then that he came to the forefront as a church leader and spokesman. Having already raised some eyebrows by bringing in two young women as research assistants, Lolek proceeded further to distress the more conservative elements in the Catholic hierarchy by delivering a speech that stressed the importance of the faithful over the clergy. He also advocated revising the Vatican's strict policies on censorship, which eventually led to works of such writers as Emmanuel Kant, John Milton, and Daniel Defoe being removed from the Index of Forbidden Books and made available for Catholics to read.

But the issue that thrust Lolek more forcefully into public scrutiny was ecumenism, or the relation of the Church to other denominations and faiths. For Lolek, it was clear that the Church needed to take a stronger stand in defense of human rights and to concern itself with the welfare of all people, not just Catholics. The Church, he argued, also needed to reach out to those of other denominations and faiths in order not to remain isolated from the world at large. In a speech given before the Council on October 21, 1964, Lolek stated, "The Church should speak so that the world sees that we are not so much teaching…but rather acting, along with the world, seeking a…just solution to difficult human problems."[4] This speech became the foundation for his papacy.

When the Council adjourned in November, Lolek made another trip to the Holy Land and then, before returning to Kraków, stopped once more in Rome where he met privately with Paul VI. The visit marked the beginning of a very special friendship between the two men as well as another important step toward the papacy.

The tumultuous final session of Vatican II convened in the fall of 1965, and pitted traditionalists against progressives over such issues as religious freedom and the relation of the Church with non-Christian religions, particularly Judaism. Working closely with Austrian Cardinal Franz König and German Cardinal Augustin Bea, Lolek helped to draft various documents, including an important part of *Nostra Aetate* (In Our Time), which exonerated the Jews of their responsibility in the persecution and death of Christ. Lolek wrote that the crucifixion could not be blamed on all Jews, past or present.

Lolek was also among the group of bishops who defeated a proposal calling upon the Second Vatican Council to issue a formal condemnation of communism. Like John XXIII and Paul VI, Lolek believed that such a move would do nothing but increase hostility and tension between the East and the West. It would neither weaken nor discredit communism. As a high-ranking Catholic official in a communist country, Lolek took a realistic view of the matter. Although staunchly anti-Communist, Lolek thought it politic to refrain from supporting such a measure, an outlook that many Western European and North American clergy did not understand.

For the rest of 1965, Lolek once more engaged in his priestly and administrative chores, wrote new poetry, sermons, and essays, including the inspirational "Reflections on Fatherhood," and sent a steady stream of reports on the activities of the Second Vatican Council to *Tygodnik Powszcheny*. He also learned that nine years after the initial petition had been filed, Communist authorities had granted permission for the construction of a church in Nowa Huta. For Lolek, this news came as a personal victory, for he had lobbied for the new church since he had become a bishop.

CARDINAL WOJTYLA

In May of 1967, just 11 days after celebrating his 47th birthday, Lolek received a surprising piece of news: Paul VI had named him a cardinal. Lolek was not the only one surprised; many in the Catholic Church in Poland were equally taken aback. There was already one cardinal in Poland, and no one expected another would be named. Once again, Lolek's relative youth also made him an unusual candidate for the office. In appointing him, Paul VI had demonstrated his respect not only for Lolek but also for his ideas about the Church. On June 28, 1967, the pope invested Archbishop Wojtyla, along with 26 other members of the clergy in the red robes of the cardinal, in a ceremony held at the Sistine Chapel in Rome. The following afternoon, Cardinal Wojtyla and the other new cardinals helped the pope celebrate Mass in Saint Peter's Square.

Elevation to cardinal proved a defining event in Lolek's life, if for no other reason than it gave him a seat in the College of Cardinals, the governing body of the Church among whose responsibilities is the election of the pope. For Lolek, the rewards of the red cap went even further. Cardinals wielded extraordinary power within their own nations. As Archbishop of Kraków, Lolek had already had a great deal of influence. As a cardinal, he was unquestionably the second most powerful Church leader in Poland, though some believed that his influence exceeded that of Wyszyński. Still, out of respect for the cardinal, Lolek never tried to challenge or supersede his decisions.

Instead, he occupied himself by attending to his new duties, transforming the archdiocese into what some called a "minipapacy."[5] Continuing to work at a frenetic pace, Lolek sought new ways to bring the message of the Second Vatican Council to his people. He also wished to build up Kraków's reputation as a leading cultural and intellectual center not only in Poland, but throughout Europe as well. All of these activities had to be undertaken with the utmost caution, for Lolek knew that the Communist authorities were never far away and were keeping a constant watch on him.

Despite monitoring Lolek's every move, the Communists still had not quite figured out who exactly he was. In a top-secret dossier compiled in 1967, the police set out their strategy of driving a wedge between the Cardinals Wojtyla and Wyszyński. The report, entitled, "Our Tactics towards Cardinals Wojtyla and Wyszyński," offers a curious interpretation of the two leading Polish churchmen. Among the information contained in the document was an assessment of Cardinal Wyszyński, which described the cardinal as having feelings of inferiority because of his traditional family background. In addition, the cardinal's approach in dealing with the communist authorities tended to be one of making concessions as well as making whatever arrangements necessary to keep both Communists and Catholics happy.

Surprisingly, Cardinal Wojtyla fared much better in the Communists' analysis. According to the same document, because Lolek came from a family of intelligentsia—making him one of the few intellectuals in the Polish Episcopate—his views on political issues were weaker and he was in general overintellectualized. The report also noted Lolek's lack of organizing and leadership qualities, something that made him, in the report's eyes, weaker than Wyszyński.

The report concluded with a list of recommendations on how to deal with the two men by demonstrating ill-will toward Wyszyński, but not so much that it would force Wojtyla to side with him. Little did the Communists realize that Lolek was already making plans to step up his crusade for the rights of the Church.

A NEW TITLE, BUT OLD WAYS

Despite his added workload and new office, Lolek continued to live in much the same way as he ever had. Every morning he rose early and said

Mass at seven o'clock in the small chapel of the archbishop's residence. Instead of working in his roomy office, Lolek worked in a small area just behind the chapel altar that contained only a red padded prayer kneeler, a small wooden desk, and a red upholstered chair. At eleven o'clock, he left his "office" and began the long round of meetings with people from all walks of life. As often as he could, Lolek made a point of seeing everyone whether or not they had an appointment with him.

By late afternoon, Lolek retired to the chapel once more where he often prayed and meditated for several hours. After dinner, Lolek continued to work or meet with people. In addition, he performed marriages, baptisms, funerals, and when possible, visited the sick and the infirm. At the end of the day, instead of sleeping in the more spacious master bedroom of the residence, he retired to a small back room.

His love of the outdoors and vigorous exercise was in no way diminished. He got away whenever he could to ski and hike in the mountains. To one reporter who visited his office, Lolek, looking up from the work piled on his desk, sighed, "I wish I could be out there now, somewhere in the mountains, racing down into a valley; it's an extraordinary sensation."[6]

Lolek's refusal to show off his position was the source of numerous amusing stories among his friends and acquaintances. On one occasion when an American woman on a skiing holiday injured her leg, Lolek serenaded her and several other skiers as she waited for medical attention. The woman never realized that her guitar-playing companion was Cardinal Wojtyla. While staying at a mountain retreat, Lolek met an elderly retired priest. Thinking Lolek was only a novice, the older man constantly asked him to run errands for him, such as getting him tea or bringing him a sweater. Lolek was happy to comply, never revealing who he was. On yet another occasion, the police detained Lolek at a mountain checkpoint for hours. Suspicious of his tattered appearance, the police thought he had stolen the archbishop's credentials that he showed them.

The subject of Lolek's appearance either brought smiles or grimaces. Many cardinals flaunted their position by wearing expensive cassocks and clothing. Lolek, by contrast, was content to wear his worn priestly garb. At times, his appearance was so shabby that even his driver complained to the diocese about his attire, stating that "His cassock is all shiny, he wears a battered hat, and his shirts have been mended over and over."[7] Another priest remembered that "For many years, he wore just one green coat. If somebody bought him a new coat, he gave it away."[8] Lolek did the same with other gifts of clothing given to him, but he never looked unkempt;

his appearance was always neat. Many in the Church compared his simple wardrobe favorably to that of Cardinal Wyszyński, who wore more ornate and expensively tailored cassocks and vestments.

Beyond his appearance, what many remembered about Lolek during his early years as cardinal was his growing commitment to the faith, combined with the determination to deal with the realities of the modern world. One of his former students recalled how Lolek:

> never feared the confrontation between theology and the world. He regularly invited people from various fields in the humanities and sciences. He knew all the important experts in literature, history, and physics. He always wanted to know what was new. He was interested in the structure of matter and the new moral problems created by advances in medicine.[9]

In an era when Catholic churchmen ignored or denigrated ideas and developments in science, the humanities, and the arts, Lolek tried to meet the world head on. He listened to the experts, but in the end, kept his own counsel and made up his own mind. This ability became increasingly important in the months ahead, as Lolek began to play an expanded role in national and Church affairs, emerging as one of the foremost champions of human rights and reform in the Roman Catholic Church.

NOTES

1. Jonathan Kwitney, *Man of the Century: The Life and Times of Pope John Paul II* (New York: Henry Holt, 1997), p. 181.

2. Ibid.

3. Ibid., p. 184.

4. Robert Sullivan, *Pope John Paul II: A Tribute* (New York: Time, 1999), p. 55.

5. Tad Szulc, *Pope John Paul II: The Biography* (New York: Scribner, 1995), p. 240.

6. Kwitney, p. 212.

7. Ibid.

8. Ibid.

9. Ibid., p. 214.

Chapter 8

THE YEAR OF THREE POPES

The friendship between Lolek and Pope Paul VI was forged out of mutual respect and a genuine liking of each other. Over the next few years, Paul increasingly began to seek Lolek's counsel on a number of Church matters. The pope also named Lolek to head up four Vatican congregations: Clergy, Catholic Education, Liturgy, and Oriental Churches, which are similar to cabinet departments in secular governments. In addition, Paul VI appointed Lolek as consultant to the Council for the Laity. But certainly one of the most important collaborations between the two came in 1968 with the pope's issue of *Humanae Vitae*, or *On Human Life*, which outlined the Church's stand on birth control.

ON HUMAN LIFE

The Papal Commission for the Study of Problems of the Family, Population, and Birth Rate was created by Pope John XXIII to study family issues and the Church. But given the growing concerns of many Catholics about the Church's stand on birth control, Paul VI reconvened the group once more to take another look at the issues.

For many Catholics, the primary question was whether the Church would allow the use of contraceptives, such as birth control pills, as a means of family planning. In Church teachings, any form of contraception other than the rhythm method, a method of birth control in which abstinence is practiced during a woman's ovulation period, was outlawed. For many Catholics by the 1960s, this outlook was outdated and unrealistic; they were hoping that the Church would change its mind. Given the climate of the times, in which it was becoming more acceptable to challenge authority along with the growing emphasis on women's reproductive rights, the Vatican was looking at a potential firestorm over the issue of birth control.

By 1966, the Papal Commission had shown itself to be of two minds. The majority of the Commission believed it was time to change the Catholic Church's position that contraception was immoral. They argued that if the Church did not change its position, it would lose its credibility with married couples and the modern world. An equally vocal minority believed the Church needed to maintain its stand on birth control. This group believed that by changing current Church teachings, the Church stood to lose its authority by admitting that for centuries it had made a mistake.

While the debate between the two factions raged, Lolek was hard at work preparing a paper that enunciated his views on birth control, which he had earlier explored in *Love and Responsibility*. Once again Lolek emphasized that the Church must maintain its stand on birth control; to lift it or modify it in any way devalued procreation and the act of intercourse between married people, and diminished the dignity of women. The paper, which took about four months to prepare, was then sent to Paul VI.

Soon it would be time for the Commission to take a vote, and both sides looked to their pope for some indication of what he was thinking. But for Paul, it was not so simple; during the next two years he wrestled with the problem, unsure of which way to turn. By 1968, he was facing increasing pressure from both sides to take a stand. The laity and some members of the clergy wished him to relax the ban, while several cardinals, including Lolek, asked that Paul keep the Church's ban on birth control in place.

In the end, Lolek's persuasive arguments helped Paul make his decision. In his heart, Paul knew that the ban needed to be kept; after studying Lolek's materials, he was even more convinced. In mid-July of 1968, Paul issued *Humanae Vitae*, which stated that the Church's position on birth control would not change. This meant that any artificial means of birth control was forbidden, as were abortions.

Humanae Vitae emerged as one of the most controversial documents issued by the Church since World War II. The document ignited a firestorm from Catholics, particularly those in the United States. The ban on contraceptive devices put some Catholics in a deeply troubling dilemma: Should they disobey Church teachings in order to limit the size of their families, or risk having more children who would be either unwanted or unaffordable? While statistics are unavailable, even at the Vatican officials believed that many Catholics simply ignored the pope's decision.

Back in Poland, Lolek showed his support for the Church's position, defending the pope whenever he could. He also organized special "*Humanae Vitae* marriage groups" in his Kraków diocese to help married couples. Using instruction and discussion, Lolek worked at helping couples honor their commitment to their faith and their marriage vows by respecting the encyclical. Lolek never once questioned his own commitment to *Humanae Vitae*; in fact, as time went on, the doctrine became an even more deeply felt part of Lolek's moral and religious beliefs.

To some, Lolek's support of the pope's encyclical seemed inconsistent with his actions in his own diocese where he had established a marriage institute that dealt with issues such as family planning, illegitimate births, venereal disease, alcoholism, and spousal and child abuse. But those who knew Lolek were quick to point out that his establishing the institute showed a deep awareness of the realities of the modern world and its problems. His firm support of the *Humanae Vitae* simply demonstrated Lolek's view of how the world could be made to be more humane.

NEW CHALLENGES

Upon returning to Kraków, Lolek resumed his duties, while taking on new projects. In 1969, he published *Person and Act*, in which he responded to Marxist teachings against religion and the Church. He also tackled the complex question of man and morality. *Person and Act* was considered such difficult reading that even priests joked that if one of the priests was sentenced to Purgatory, he would be sprung free upon reading the entire text. When Lolek heard the comment, friends reported that his response was the closest thing to a belly laugh they had ever seen from him.

On a cold February evening in 1969, Lolek surprised many Catholic citizens with a visit to a Jewish synagogue in Kazimierz, the Jewish district in Kraków. Nobody in Poland could ever remember a Catholic cardinal

going to visit a Jewish synagogue. For Lolek, the gesture was both a symbolic and genuine attempt to bring about some reconciliation between
the two faiths. In going to the synagogue, Lolek was also pursuing something he had fought long and hard for as cardinal: the removal of blame
from Jews for Christ's death. Accompanied by a parish priest from a
nearby neighborhood, Lolek entered the temple with his head covered, as
was customary. He then met quietly with some of the city's Jewish leaders
before entering the synagogue where the congregation was holding
prayers. Standing silently at the back, Lolek listened to the service.

That same year, Lolek also turned his attention to what he believed
were some overdue projects. As one of his first acts as cardinal, he ordered
the restoration of the Wawel Cathedral, now seven centuries old. His actions demonstrated again the deep love he had for his country and his
church. When the tomb of Queen Elżbieta, one of Poland's most famous
sovereigns, was discovered under a pile of rubble, Lolek authorized the
opening of the tomb and the re-burial of the queen's remains, along with
the remains of her husband, King Kazmierz the Great. Ever fascinated by
the relationship between science, technology, and history, Lolek gave permission for microbiological tests to be done on the interiors of the royal
crypts.

GROOMING A FUTURE POPE

By 1969, Pope Paul VI realized that if Lolek were to continue in his
role as a church leader, he needed to broaden his experience. He decided
that Lolek should begin traveling to meet with Church and lay leaders
throughout the world. This would not only broaden his scope, but educate
him further in the skills of diplomacy he needed to represent the Church.

Lolek's first trip was to North America, where he visited Polish com-
munities, marking the first time that a Polish cardinal had visited North
America. On August 26, 1969, Lolek, his chaplain, and two friends, left
Rome and flew first to Montreal. For the next three weeks, they toured
Canada, visiting many of the major cities. Lolek met with many Polish-
Canadian clergy, celebrated Mass in Polish at Polish churches, and went
to numerous lunches, receptions, and dinners at Polish-Canadian
parishes. He also met with the country's primate and many of the leading
Canadian bishops.

Leaving Canada, Lolek traveled to Niagara Falls and Buffalo, New
York, for a two-week visit to the United States. The Vatican advised
Lolek to visit every major American city where cardinals had sees, or gov-

erning offices. As a result, Lolek went to Detroit, Boston, Washington, D.C., Baltimore, St. Louis, Chicago, Philadelphia, and New York, as well as other cities where there were no cardinals in residence. For the most part, his trip to the United States was similar to his visit in Canada, as he made the rounds of Polish-Catholic communities in most every city he visited, celebrated Mass, and met with Church and government leaders.

His trip to North America, while not terribly inclusive, as he was there on behalf of the Polish communities who had invited him, did teach Lolek quite a bit about North American social niceties. Father Szcepan Wesoly, who accompanied Lolek on this trip remembered Lolek's initial response to American cocktail parties. At first, Lolek disliked participating in this American ritual, then realized that it might be a good idea because it allowed a person to chat, whether they drank or not, unlike in Poland where one just downed his or her vodka. Lolek also looked forward to the many dinners and banquets, for they afforded him an opportunity to converse with others; similarly, press conferences were good, as Lolek's English began improving with each one he participated in. One special event marked Lolek's visit. While in Philadelphia, the cardinal asked Lolek whether he would like to visit Doylestown, Pennsylvania, where a large number of Polish Americans lived. Lolek made the trip by helicopter, which was the first time he had ever traveled so. According to those who accompanied him, he loved it. In October, Lolek left the United States and returned to Rome. For the most part, he seemed pleased with the trip. He later reported that the Poles in North America had done well in maintaining their spiritual link with Poland and with the Church. He was also pleased with his reception by the American bishops and cardinals whom he had met.

When Lolek next returned to the United States, he came as pope. He never again had the opportunity to mingle with the American people and get to know them. His first visit, while successful, may have thus contributed to his unfavorable view of the United States years later. In one interview with the Polish *Tygodnik Powszechny,* Lolek suggested that one of the problems with American society was its lack of identification with the idea of an American nation. For Lolek, Americans lacked conviction when speaking of an American nation, unlike Poles, who strongly identified with Poland and a Polish nation.

Lolek made another international trip in 1973, spending February on a tour of Australia, New Zealand, Papua New Guinea, with a brief stop in the Philippines. Never one to waste time, even during plane flights, Lolek kept a detailed travel diary that, when finished, was the size of a book.

During his visit, Lolek made a favorable impression on the cardinals and bishops whom he met, even making some new friends among them. As a result of his two journeys, Lolek had the urge to travel even more extensively, a desire he fulfilled as pope.

FIGHTING THE REGIME

In between his journeys, Lolek focused his attention on a series of events in his homeland. With his ascension to cardinal, Lolek was determined to fight the Communist regime in any way he could. In a sermon delivered in Sandomierz, in southeastern Poland on June 8, 1968, Lolek reminded his listeners of the earlier Russian occupation of Poland during the nineteenth century. He also spoke of the Catholic clergy's obligation to not allow the Catholic Church to become "Russified," a veiled reference to the Russian Orthodox Church, the national church of Russia. He also informed his audience of the importance of a unified Church in the history of Poland.

Much of Lolek's sermon was in reference to an earlier incident. Almost three months before, students in Warsaw took to the streets in protest after attending the strongly patriotic and very anti-Russian play *The Forefathers' Eve*. Riots broke out on the University of Warsaw campus as well as in several of the city's neighborhoods. In retaliation, the Gomulka government launched an anti-Semitic campaign in which almost every Jewish person was fired from any government or teaching job.

The events of March marked the slow demise of the Gomulka government. Gomulka had fully embraced Soviet policies. Many Poles were still angry over Gomulka's decision to send Polish troops to help quell the political unrest in Czechoslovakia a year earlier. Then in December of 1970, Gomulka called out the army and security troops to stop rioting workers in Gdańsk, a prominent port city located on the Baltic Sea. The workers were demanding better living conditions and were also protesting the rising price of food. Tanks fired on the workers and several were killed.

In response to the episode, the Soviet government in Moscow replaced Gomulka with Edward Gierek, a career party official who was considered a more moderate political leader. While Gierek's government did little to change the ever-present Communist pressure on the Church, it did nothing to escalate it either, knowing how stubborn and powerful the Polish clergy could be.

While deeply saddened by the events that had transpired at Gdańsk, Lolek was a realist when it came to dealing with life in a Communist country. He denounced the Gdańsk killings in no uncertain terms, and demanded "the right to bread, the rights to freedom...a climate of real liberty...[and] freedom from fear."[1]

When Gierek came to power, Lolek continued to carry on his never-ending battle of wills with the government. In 1973 for instance, Lolek requested the building of 77 churches. Sixteen were built. He lobbied hard for the abolition of compulsory military service for seminary students; in response, the government drafted only half of those eligible. These were small victories perhaps, but victories nonetheless. Lolek also continued to speak out in sermons for the right of religious freedom, particularly in regard to giving children Catholic instruction. While Communist authorities fumed, there was little they could do except hope that Lolek would make a mistake and land in greater trouble. Lolek, though, continued his policy of negotiating and compromising with authorities, and becoming tough only when necessary to protect the Church and the nation.

SPECIAL RECOGNITION

In the aftermath of *Humanae Vitae*, Paul VI and Lolek became even closer. Between 1973 and 1975, the pope invited Lolek into his study for eleven private audiences, where the two met and talked. In 1976, the pope honored Lolek even further by extending him an invitation to deliver the annual Lenten spiritual exercises at the Vatican. But the invitation had been extended late, leaving Lolek with only three weeks to prepare.

His presentation given in March, 1976, was entitled "Meditations," and would later be published under the title, *A Sign of Contradiction*. Speaking in Italian, Lolek's presentation was a personal manifesto of sorts in which he outlined his view of the world and defined the Church's moral and ethical role within it. Although Lolek had expressed many of these ideas before, this was a very different situation. It was clear to many in the room that Paul VI was in failing health. Gathered before Lolek were the men who were charged with the responsibility of choosing the next pope. What they did not know was that Paul VI had asked Lolek to make his presentation in Italian rather than Latin to demonstrate to the group his grasp of the language and to show that he could handle himself if elected pope. It was the closest Paul could get to revealing his choice of a successor. But others had noticed the new cardinal from Poland, too; that same year, the *New York Times* placed Lolek's name on the list of the ten candidates to succeed Pope Paul VI.

Lolek's thoughts, however, were occupied not with the papacy, but with events in his country. In June of 1976, the government, not remembering the event in Gdańsk, raised food prices again. The move provoked government workers to riot near Warsaw and other cities. Soon after, the railway workers also went on strike. Not wishing to exacerbate the situation, the government canceled the proposed price increases.

Lolek and Cardinal Wyszyński implored the workers to return to their jobs and asked the government not to punish the protestors. While peace was restored, a new organization, KOR, the Polish acronym for the Committee for the Defense of Workers, was created. The organization marked the first time a functioning political alliance had been established between Polish workers and intellectuals. Lolek soon established his own ties with the group, as did the Catholic Intellectuals Clubs (KIK) and the more progressive wing of the Catholic Church. These groups, in turn, later influenced the emergence of another workers' group: Solidarity.

In May 1977, Lolek had the satisfaction of consecrating a new church in the workers' suburb of Nowa Huta, built earlier as a model "socialist city." The building of the new church came after years of struggle, and signaled the growing closeness between the Gierek government and the Church. Although the permit had been issued in 1967, years of harassment by the government had made construction painfully slow. One indication of these new relations came in September when Lolek traveled to Rome to meet with the pope about arranging an important visit. That December, President Gierek was received by Pope Paul VI, making him the first Polish Communist leader to be granted an audience with the pope.

TRAGIC NEWS

On May 19, 1978, Lolek called on the pope before leaving Rome. Little did either man realize that it would be the last time they talked. Lolek then left for a long vacation. He was quite tired and had not completely recovered from earlier illness and debilitating migraine headaches. Then on August 6, 1978, came the news: Pope Paul VI had died at his summer residence at Castel Gandolfo, after suffering a heart attack during Mass. Those at the pope's house have said that at the precise moment of the pope's death, the buzzer on an small alarm clock that he had bought during a visit to Poland sixty years ago went off. While people were saddened at the news, it was not a great surprise, for the pope had been in failing health for some time.

It was now up to the College of Cardinals, which was to gather in three weeks, to elect a new pope. Lolek, along with Cardinal Wyszyński, left for Rome on August 12. They would attend the pope's funeral and later the conclave to pick his successor. On August 25, 1978, the 111 cardinals gathered at the Vatican to begin the selection process. Only 11 had ever been through the process before, but even before Paul's death, speculation and rumors abounded over who would be the next pope. In the weeks before Paul's death, bishops and priests had passed on dossiers of candidates they liked and those they did not. In some cases, the documents contained accusations such as dishonesty in financial dealings or violation of the vow of celibacy. The cardinals were expressly forbidden to campaign for their favorite, though messages were often passed containing secretly worded meanings about possible candidates.

Supervising the selection process was Cardinal Jean Villot of France. Every morning he organized formal meetings made up of small groups. Generally speaking, the talk during these meetings was much freer as there was no pope to oversee the cardinals. Here the cardinals talked of a wide range of issues concerning the Church, including the role of the Church in Communist-bloc countries such as Poland. Lolek attended these morning meetings, though he spent his afternoons at a rented house near the seashore.

In order to elect a pope, 75 cardinals, or a two-thirds plus one majority, was needed. All of the favored candidates were Italian, and long-standing members of the Curia. None were considered too radical, so any changes in Church policy would be minimal, particularly after the transitions and reforms made during the papacies of John XXIII and Paul VI. Although everyone assumed the next pope would be Italian, there were some, like Cardinal Silvio Oddi, who thought otherwise: "I was one of the cardinals already thinking that the nationality of the pope does not necessarily have to be Italian." After talking with Cardinal Wojtyla, Oddi thought of Cardinal Wyszyński as a possible candidate. "But Wyszyński was very old. And thinking of Wyszyński brought to mind another Pole."[2]

CHOOSING A POPE

The cardinals met in the Sistine Chapel. During their deliberations, they were quarantined in a sealed and draped area near the chapel, where they would stay until they came to a decision. One priest who has witnessed the papal selection process described the conditions under which the cardinals worked:

The plastic dining room chairs look like a discount-store bar-
gain sale. The rugs they put in the Sistine Chapel...are cheap
felt and will be filthy after the first group of cardinals walks
down the aisle to vote. Each cardinal is issued one roll of toilet
paper, two ballpoint pens...and maybe ten sheets of writing
paper.... Each also gets a plastic wastebasket out of a dime
store, a washbowl and pitcher, a red plastic glass, a tiny bed
lamp, one hard-backed chair and even harder-looking [prayer]
kneeler. To make it clear that he ought to get out in a hurry, he
gets only one bar of soap and two very tiny towels, which will
drive the Americans up the wall.... The beds are the worst I
think I've seen since seminary...very narrow, with thin, hard
mattresses over wire mesh.[3]

While many cardinals may have had a hard time adapting to these circumstances, this environment was nothing out of the ordinary for Lolek,
who was used to sparse rooms and few belongings.

When it came time to begin deliberations, the cardinals were crowded
among the chairs and tables. They were then handed a card printed with
the Latin phrase, *Eligo in summum pontificem,* or "I chose as supreme pontiff." The cardinals were told to disguise their handwriting and fold the
card over to hide their vote. Then, in order of seniority, each one moved
to the chapel altar, knelt, prayed, rose, and then announced, "I call to witness Christ, the Lord, who will be my judge that my vote is given to the
one who, before God, I consider should be elected." Then the folded card
was placed on a plate and slid into a chalice. The cardinal bowed and returned to his seat. Three cardinals tallied the vote. The whole process was
over in about an hour, and on average, was repeated twice a day until a
new pope was selected. At the end of each round of voting, the ballots
were burned. Onlookers in St. Peter's Square could keep track of the conclave's progress. Black smoke from the Vatican chimney signaled there
had been no decision. When a new pope was elected, a special chemical
was added to the ballots, turning the smoke white.

Early into the voting, the cardinal most favored to become pope was
Giuseppe Siri, who had lobbied hard against significant reforms and was
considered to be very conservative. But he did not have a majority to win.
Clearly the conclave was looking for someone who would consider
change, but not push hard for it. Lolek received a few votes, but did not
think for one moment that he would be chosen. While he knew that Paul
VI had groomed him to become the first non-Italian pope, he also believed that his time had not yet come: at least not as long as there were acceptable Italian candidates. In the end, a compromise candidate, Cardinal

Albino Luciani, the archbishop of Venice, the son of a migrant worker and maid, was chosen as the new pope. His election also signaled an end to the recent string of popes like Paul VI who through family connections had spent their careers ascending the Church hierarchy.

When asked by which name he wished to be called, the new pope made an unusual decision. He wished to honor his predecessors who, through reform and restraint, had guided the Church during the tumultuous years of the mid-twentieth century. And so, the new pope took the name John Paul I. One of the first visitors he received was Cardinal Wojtyla of Poland.

AN OVERWHELMING JOB

It seemed almost from the beginning that the cardinals might have made a mistake in their selection. While the new pope was friendly, open to discussion, and willing to listen, he appeared overwhelmed by his new duties. He lacked the needed administrative experience and his assistants were as lost as he was. Equally disturbing was the pope's reaction when faced with the mounting paperwork. He simply did not know where to start.

Complicating matters was the pope's health. A long-standing circulatory problem had worsened to the point where he could no longer wear shoes. The pope, too, seemed plagued by bad luck: when the head of the Russian Orthodox Church, Archbishop Nikodim came to visit, he fell dead at the pope's feet. On another occasion, the pope was walking on the rooftop garden of the Vatican to help his circulation when he lost important and confidential papers as a gust of wind blew them from his hand. The incident sent the Vatican Guard leaping from rooftop to rooftop in order to retrieve them.

While Vatican officials were concerned about John Paul I, they did not take any steps to monitor his physical condition. His medical records were in transit from Venice and a doctor in Rome had not yet received them. This seeming indifference to the pontiff's health was the source of much criticism later on, as Vatican officials were accused of maintaining their shroud of secrecy and privacy at the expense of the pope's well-being.

THE POPE IS DEAD

At 4:30 A.M., on September 29, 1978, Sister Vincenzina brought the pope his morning coffee just as she did every morning. She left the cup outside his door; when she returned a half hour later, the cup was still there. Alarmed, she entered the pope's bedroom to find John Paul I curled up on his right side, his hand clutching some papers. He was dead. The news left the Vatican reeling. John Paul I's tenure had been a mere 34 days, the shortest reign of a pope since Leo XI's ten-day rule during the seventeenth century.

Vatican officials decided not to reveal that the pope had been discovered in his pajamas by a woman. As one Vatican official later stated, "The world cannot be told that a woman was the first person to enter the pontiff's bedroom."[4] An official announcement broadcast over Vatican Radio at 7:42 that morning announced the pope's death, stating that the body had been found by the Monsignor John Magee, the pope's Secretary of State. Even though rumors circulated that the pope had died as a result of foul play, the official cause of death was given as a heart attack. This was not implausible, given the overall poor health of John Paul I.

At the time of the John Paul I's death, Lolek was celebrating the twentieth anniversary of his consecration as bishop by presiding over the opening of the Wawel Cathedral Museum. He learned of the news at breakfast, the following morning. He went about his day's work quietly, participating in a meeting and visiting a parish. On his return home, Lolek asked the driver to stop so he could finish writing letters on his lap desk. Lolek, upon returning to his quarters, instructed an assistant to have the letters typed up and sent. As the assistant recalled, it was as if Lolek wanted to take care of all his affairs, not leaving anything undone or overlooked. On October 3, 1978, Lolek and Cardinal Wyszyński again boarded a plane for Rome to choose a new pope.

A BREAK WITH HISTORY

In one of the last decrees that Paul VI handed down before his death, he eliminated cardinals over 80 years old from being considered for the papacy. This reduction in the number of eligible candidates indirectly gave rise to another intriguing possibility. Of the 111 members of the College of Cardinals who gathered in October of 1978 to elect a new pope, 56 represented countries in Western Europe. That slight majority might still have ensured the selection of a Western European—and in all likelihood an Italian—successor to John Paul I if it had been unified. The Italian cardinals, however, had broken into quarreling factions that shattered the unity of the Western European group. Given the limited number of candidates and the divisions among the Western European cardinals, the chance of electing a non-Italian pope became suddenly more realistic.

Upon Lolek's arrival in Rome, he attended the pope's funeral. In the days before the conclave was set to meet, he made the most of his time visiting friends, taking small trips to the country, and talking with other Church officials. During this time, too, Lolek was attracting more and more attention. Many cardinals started to view the cardinal from Poland in a different light.

Lolek said nothing about his own desires—if there were any—to be elected pope. But a close friend, Bishop Deskur, who organized many of the dinners and get-togethers for Lolek, believed that Lolek knew he was to become the next pope. Still, there was no telling what the conclave might do when it met.

On October 15, the conclave met at the Sistine Chapel once more to begin its deliberations, but it was clear by the end of the day that there was no clear favorite in the running. The cardinals appeared to be dead-locked between two Italian candidates: Cardinal Guiseppe Siri of Genoa and Cardinal Giovanni Benelli of Florence. Of the two, Siri, at 72, was the oldest and the most conservative, having been one of the more out-spoken critics of Vatican Council II. Benelli, who was 57, had been a close associate of Paul VI, and was considered to be more progressive in his views. The two symbolized the current struggle the Church was engaged in, between instituting reform and maintaining traditional views and practices.

When the conclave broke for the day, it was clear that there would be no Italian pope elected; the rivalry between the two factions was too much to overcome. Certain cardinals took it upon themselves to talk with others about the possibility of a non-Italian pope. It also gave the cardinals time to assess what they needed in their new pontiff. Many believed that it was important for the new pope to be a "pastoral pope," that is, one who is familiar with the workings of parishes, dioceses, and archdioceses. This was becoming more important as the changes of Vatican II were implemented and a reorganization of the Church was underway. The last several popes of the twentieth century were more skilled in Vatican diplomacy than at working with parish churches. While John Paul I had been a pastoral pope, his tenure had been too brief to accomplish anything. In Lolek Wojtyla, there seemed to be an answer, and a real possibility of continuing that legacy. Another consideration was age and health. Many believed the Church needed a younger pope, one who could guide the Church through the remaining years of the twentieth century and hopefully into the twenty-first. In the end, what the cardinals were looking for was someone young and in good health, possessed of a fine mind, pastorally experienced, with dedication to the Vatican and a good grasp of world affairs. While many thought this a tall order, there were those who already knew such a person existed.

On Monday morning, October 16, the cardinals met again. While Lolek's supporters were growing in number, they were still far from acquiring the necessary two-thirds plus one majority. Even Lolek's colleague, Cardinal Wyszyński, did not entertain Lolek's candidacy with any seriousness. He believed that if a foreign cardinal might be elected, it was to be he, not Lolek. Yet, the cardinal also believed that in the end, an Italian would be chosen, stating that it would be difficult to violate a 455-year-old tradition. Still, Lolek's old friend Cardinal König, got up and spoke before the conclave stating that in his opinion, the time had come to break with tradition, to change the system and vote for a non-Italian.

But by Monday afternoon, there was still no majority candidate. The field now consisted of four possibilities: Lolek, König (who did not want the job), Cardinal Eduardo Francisco Pironio of Argentina, and Cardinal Johannes Willebrands of the Netherlands. But slowly throughout the room, it was becoming clear that Lolek was the one. Still, at the end of the first ballot, there was no majority. Slowly, Lolek's supporters worked to bring others to his side. First came the Americans, followed by the Germans, then the Latin Americans and Africans. But the Italians were still holding out with their 25 votes.

Shortly after 5 P.M., another ballot was cast. The tension inside the chapel was palpable. Many knew that if no decision was reached, the Church was facing an overwhelming crisis. It was imperative that a candidate be elected. Finally, a break came in the form of the Italian Cardinal Sebastiano Baggio, one of the more powerful members of the Italian faction. He was followed by a number of stubborn Italian cardinals. As votes were called out, König looked over to Lolek, who, looking confused and red in the face, had put down his pencil. Then holding his head in his hands, Lolek heard the final tally: two-thirds of the vote plus one had been cast in his favor. In the end, Lolek was elected pope with 94 votes; 17 cardinals went on record refusing to accept him. When asked if he would accept the decision, Lolek replied with no hesitation, "It is God's will. I accept." Cardinal Tarancón later summed up the afternoon's events: "God forced us to break with history to elect Karol Wojtyla."[5]

Out of respect for his predecessor, Lolek took the name John Paul II. He was the 264th man to become pope. He was now head of the world's single largest Church, with approximately one billion followers, and one of the world's oldest religions. At 58 years of age, he was the youngest pope to be elected since 1846, and the first non-Italian pope since 1523. His new title was, "The Bishop of Rome, the Vicar of Jesus Christ, the Successor of St. Peter, Prince of the Apostles, the Supreme Pontiff who has the primacy of jurisdiction and not merely of honor over the Universal Church, the Patriarch of the West, the Primate of Italy, the Archbishop and Metropolitan of the Roman Province, the Sovereign of the State of Vatican City, Servant of the Servants of God." He was to be addressed as, "His Holiness the Pope," or the more informal title, "Holy Father."

As Lolek was led to a small whitewashed room where he would put on the white papal vestments, white smoke spewed out from the chimneys. Its message: a new pope had been elected and a new chapter in personal and Church history was beginning.

NOTES

1. Carl Bernstein and Marco Politi, *His Holiness: John Paul II and the Hidden History of Our Time* (New York: Doubleday, 1996), p. 113.

2. Jonathan Kwitney, *Man of the Century: The Life and Times of Pope John Paul II* (New York: Henry Holt, 1997), p. 283.

3. Ibid., p. 284.

4. Bernstein and Politi, p. 151.

5. Tad Szulc, *Pope John Paul II: The Biography* (New York: Scribner, 1995), pp. 280–281.

Chapter 9

"BEHOLD, THE SLAVIC POPE IS COMING"

As soon as he had donned the white papal vestments, Lolek was led back to the Sistine Chapel altar, where an armchair stood waiting. According to Church tradition, the new pope must sit in the chair to receive the cardinals' vows of obedience. But Lolek chose to break with tradition—the first of many—simply stating that he received his Church brothers standing up. And did so. As each cardinal approached the new pope, John Paul II embraced him. In closing the ceremony, the cardinals sang a *Te Deum*, a hymn of praise to God.

Pope John Paul II then left the chapel and walked to the Vatican Loggia, the central balcony that overlooks St. Peter's Square. By now, the area was filled with people; over 200,000 Italians, tourists, and others anxiously awaited their first glimpse of the new pope. At 6:44 P.M., Cardinal Felici, one of the early contenders for the office, stepped out onto the balcony, just as the large cross on the front of St. Peter's lit up, and the Swiss Guard, the Vatican's security, marched into the square. A band began to play and the papal flag was unfurled and snapped in the breeze. Felici greeted the audience with the words, "I announce to you a great joy.... We have a Pope!—*Habemus Papam!*" As the crowd roared, Felici waited a moment and then began again, "Carolum Sanctae Romanae Ecclesiae

Cardinalem Wojtyla," or, "Carol, Holy Roman Churchman, Cardinal Wojtyla." The crowd fell silent. Who was this new pope? No one seemed to recognize the name. Some asked if the new pope was African. "No," someone in the crowd yelled, "He's Polish!"[1]

THE POLISH POPE

As John Paul II moved to the front of the balcony, he looked down upon the crowd and smiled. The next few moments proved important in determining whether the people would accept a non-Italian pope. Instead of bestowing the traditional first blessing upon the crowd, Lolek broke with tradition again. He delivered a brief message in Italian that he had composed during the balloting when he realized that he was going to be the next pope, asking among other things for the crowd's forgiveness of his poor Italian. At this, the crowd laughed and applauded. It was clear that this pope was very different from others. His presence was strong and his movements were bold, like an actor's. His voice rang clear and confident, not at all like the quiet reserve and singsong rhythms of Paul VI or the unassuming and quiet demeanor of John Paul I. When Lolek explained he had taken the name John Paul II in honor of the three popes who preceded him, he knew the crowd approved of his choice. Their enthusiastic reception was a sign of how the world would react to this new pope and extraordinary man.

The following day, October 17, was John Paul II's first full day as the new pontiff. He started the day by celebrating Mass in the morning. That afternoon he paid a visit to his friend, the ailing Bishop Deskur, who had suffered a stroke. As a crowd gathered in the clinic's corridor waiting to be blessed, the new pope smiled self-consciously and remarked that he was not used to his new duties yet. Later that day, he received his Polish friends in an informal ceremony that John Paul II called, "Farewell to the Motherland." Each person was granted a few moments with their friend. Among the first to be called were Jerzy Kluger (Lolek's childhood friend) and his wife. That evening, the pope ordered his cardinal's red skullcap to be placed at the altar of the Polish Virgin of Ostrabrana in Vilnius, in what was then Soviet Lithuania. In order for the cap to be taken to its destination safely, it had to be smuggled into the country in order to escape the ever-watchful eyes of the Soviet authorities.

If Rome was still unconvinced about the worthiness of her new pope, Poland was awash in a sea of joy and amazement. On the day of Pope John Paul II's investiture, or inauguration, as pope, 90 percent of the country's population watched the events on television. It was as if the country stopped for a day. Hotels opened their lobbies so people could come in to watch the proceedings. Masses were postponed so parishioners could stay at home to see the festivities. Carmelite friars, a monastic order that shuns all contact with the outside world, broke their vows against watching television to see the new pope ordained. For only the second time since World War II, the bells of the 450-year-old Royal Castle Cathedral in Kraków, Poland rang; the first time had been when John Paul II had been elected pope. The Communist authorities in Poland faced an impossible situation. As one party official commented: "A Pole has become Pope. It is a great event for the Polish people and a great complication for us."[2]

"THEY WILL NOT TELL ME WHAT TO DO"

The new pope's first hundred days in office set the tone for how things were to be done at the Vatican. During the rather chilly winter in Rome, he ordered the windows kept open, leaving his cold associates grumbling about "Polish air conditioning." As for the pope, he wore a cardigan sweater between his cassock and his cape and enjoyed taking in the air. His assistants and other clerics often had to run to keep up with John Paul II, as he strode down the halls much as he would a crossing path in the Polish foothills.

There were other changes, too. When a young prelate told John Paul II that his job was to tell the him when he had spoken too long in public, the pontiff retorted, "I'm the pope and I know how to behave."[3] The Swiss Guard was warned to keep his distance when Lolek took his walks. The Curia, the Vatican bureaucracy, were also told in no uncertain terms not to push John Paul II around, as he would push back. As the pope later commented to a friend, "The Curia told my predecessor what he should do and when. This may have led to his death. They will not tell *me* what to do. I will decide. They will not kill me."[4]

This pope meant business. He worked eighteen-hour days, scheduling many meetings during the course of an afternoon; many of his predecessors could hardly handle one. He had guests for most every meal, instead of eating alone or with his secretary. Vatican diplomats could expect to be grilled about local conditions and were supposed to be able to answer the pope's questions. But the pope could also be unpredictable. To the horror of the Swiss Guard who was assigned to protect him, he would plunge suddenly into crowds to shake hands and bless the small children that were held up to him. People waiting for him in the corridors of the Vatican could expect him to stop and say a few words. To the faithful, he was always accessible and interested. For those who worked with him, the pope rarely provided a dull moment.

A NEW PATH

It was becoming quite clear to those around him that the new pope was not an "accidental pope" who might make up things as he went along. He had a clear understanding of his office, and an even clearer agenda. He was prepared to exercise compassion when needed and toughness when required. As the pope's friend and confidante Bishop Deskur recalled, everything that the new pope had endured in his earlier life had prepared him for this moment.

John Paul II became pope at a time when the Roman Catholic Church was floundering within. This internal crisis sparked defections of Roman Catholics the world over who found the Church's teachings out-of-date and unrealistic. Priests and nuns were leaving their offices, further compounding an already shrinking number of men and women in the Church's religious vocations. To complicate matters, the Church was losing influence among the laity and clergy who remained in the fold. If the Church was to retain its position in the world and maintain its own institutions, then someone had to step up and lead.

Accepting this massive responsibility, John Paul II moved swiftly to impose strict discipline on the Church, including the Curia and the Church worldwide. This strategy was nothing new; it comprised many of the same principles and ideas that the pope had implemented over the 10-year period he had served as cardinal in Kraków, and through his work with Paul VI. He would, in effect, restore the absolute rule of the papacy, which had been weakened over the years. In doing so, he placed the Church squarely within the world forum, both in religious and secular affairs.

During his first months in office, John Paul II showed the direction he hoped to take. He told the clergy in Rome not to water down their messages to their parishioners by showing an exaggerated interest in social problems and neglecting the spiritual aspects of their mission. He championed celibacy among priests and the unmarried. He asked American bishops to be more watchful about upholding Catholic doctrine and discipline. He emphasized at a conference of nuns the importance of wearing the religious habit over street clothes, for it was a symbol "to remind [them] of [their] commitment, which sharply contrasts with the spirit of the world."[5] He also stressed the same principle to priests who preferred not to wear the cassock and collar. To Canadian bishops, he stressed the need to maintain individual confession of sins rather than offering general absolution. He reminded members of the Vatican Secretariat for the Union of Christians that if the ecumenical movement were to succeed, it must never compromise the truth of Church teachings, a key theme echoed throughout John Paul II's papacy .

He praised mothers who refused to have abortions even when childbirth put their lives at risk, and sternly criticized the Italian government for legalizing abortions. When a woman journalist asked him about the possibility of the Church allowing women priests, the pope bluntly replied, "The Virgin preferred to stand at the foot of the Cross."[6] He criticized the easy availability of divorce and stressed the importance of marriage vows. In the meantime, the new pope continued to make headlines around the world. He was named as one of *People* magazine's 25 most intriguing people for 1978, sharing the distinction with celebrities such as Brooke Shields, Farrah Fawcett, John Travolta, and President Jimmy Carter. John Paul II had no comment on his selection.

WORLD TRAVELER

Another break with old policy came in the pope's insistence on making the Vatican a player in world affairs. This reversal ended a century of dispute between the Church's religious and secular pursuits. The Vatican now became a modern nation-state that sought to establish diplomatic ties with nations around the world.

Beginning in 1979, John Paul II began the first of many trips around the world, continuing a tradition begun by Paul VI. As a roving ambassador for the Catholic Church, John Paul II hoped to implement his plan of religious and political diplomacy. In January, he left for Puebla, Mexico, to attend a conference of the Latin American episcopate that Paul VI had promised to attend. It was the first time Lolek had ever visited Latin America. The trip also marked his first encounter with the Theology of Liberation. This religious and political philosophy suggested cooperation was necessary with leftist groups if social justice were to prevail. With many Latin American countries under rigid and oppressive right-wing control, Liberation Theology was a form of militant social protest, an appealing alternative to traditional Catholic social doctrine to members of the clergy and laity alike.

Before leaving on his trip, the pope read everything he could about Liberation Theology, particularly the writings of the Reverend Gustavo Gutiérrez, a Peruvian priest, regarded as the founder of the movement. John Paul II understood the doctrine, but it was not to his liking. Although he favored social justice, the pope was not comfortable with members of the Church being too closely aligned with Marxist groups. Based on his own experiences with the Communist government in Poland, the pope feared that such alliances would dissolve, with the Church ending up under the control of Marxist governments. Speaking to the Latin American bishops, he stated that the idea of a political or revolutionary Jesus was not in harmony with the Church's teaching.

Even when faced with the difficult and harsh realities of Latin American Catholics living in poverty and fear, the pope could not sanction Liberation Theology. It was a bitter disappointment to those who came to the conference, as many had hoped, for the pope's support. Instead, the pope told the bishops that the Church should practice the more traditional "Option for the Poor," in that work on behalf of the poor must remain spiritually centered and avoid direct intervention in politics. The clergy must preach social reconciliation rather than class struggle. The pope's stand on Liberation Theology underscored his belief that the Church must never—under any circumstances—lose control over its own, especially in a world where the sacred and the secular were increasingly colliding.

Overall, though, despite the controversy over Liberation Theology, the pope's trip to Latin America was a success. In Mexico, a country known for its strong anti-clerical bias, people cheered as the pope's car rode by, and policemen were seen on their knees kissing the hand of the pope. When the pope's plane left Mexico City, millions gathered along the flight path and raised small mirrors to the sky, flashing their greetings to John Paul II.

The pope's trip was closely covered by the news media who discovered that the new pope did not shy away from the camera or from tough questions. One of the most memorable images was the pope's arrival in Santo Domingo, the oldest city in Hispaniola (the island that Haiti and the Dominican Republic share), and the landing site of Christopher Columbus on his first voyage to the New World. When the pope departed from his plane, he knelt down and kissed the ground, stunning onlookers and television viewers alike. It was the beginning of a new tradition that the pope carried out every time he visited a country for the first time.

THE REDEEMER OF MAN

By early March 1979, John Paul II was back in Rome. Among the many matters to which he attended, one was especially important to him: improving relations between the Church and the Jewish people. Since the mid-sixteenth century, the record of the Vatican toward the Jews had been abysmal. During the mid-sixteenth century, Pope Paul IV created what became known as the Roman Ghetto, an area created to segregate Jews from the main population, and issued a papal law that ordered Jews to live and work in this area. The law also banned non-Jews from living in the ghetto. Some years later, Pope Pius V issued another papal document that called for the banishment of the Jews from the Church territories, and recommended that all the bordering Italian states create ghettos. As a result, by the beginning of the 17th century, the majority of the major towns and cities in Italy had a Jewish ghetto. By this time, the idea of Jewish ghettos had spread throughout Europe. Even though Vatican II had formally exonerated the Jews for causing the death of Christ, the move was met with great resistance by many of the clergy.

John Paul II was determined to change this state of affairs. He invited the leaders of various Jewish organizations to the Vatican. But the meeting was destined for failure almost from the beginning. When the pope suggested that Jews fully respect the importance of Jerusalem, one of the holiest Jewish sites, to the Christian and Islamic traditions, he met with a quick and stern refusal. His other suggestion of having the UN intervene in Jerusalem to maintain religious harmony and to restore the rights of the Palestinian residents of the city were also rebuffed. Although frustrated by the meeting's outcome, the pope refused to give up his quest for repairing Jewish-Catholic relations.

Not long after this meeting, John Paul II issued his first encyclical, only five months after his election, another first for a new pope. The document, *Redemptor Hominis* or "Redeemer of Man," was a summary of his views on such topics as the moral teachings of the Church, social justice, and human rights. The timing of the encyclical was crucial as the Church's stature had suffered. In Eastern Europe, the Church had become marginalized by Communist regimes. In the West, the Church suffered from a drop in priestly vocations and an increasing spread of hostility or indifference toward the Church and many of its practices. With *Redemptor Hominis*, the pope brought a message of hope, which was central to his papacy. He stressed that material and economic progress did not automatically mean spiritual and moral growth, and criticized economic systems, from capitalism to socialism, for damaging the environment and for making poverty more widespread throughout the world. But John Paul II also stressed the dignity and greatness that is within each individual as a child of God and insisted that political systems needed to be continuously reformed in order to protect the rights of every individual.

Redemptor Hominis also emphasized the pope's belief that he was a defender of all faiths, not just Catholicism. If anywhere there were people suffering as the result of bringing God's message to others, John Paul II vowed to intervene if necessary. It was a strong position to take, but the document left little doubt as to how the pope viewed the world and what he proposed to help change it.

In other areas of the world, such as Latin America and South Africa, however, where there was clear oppression, violence, and bloodshed, the pope tended to move more slowly. He held fast to his belief that the Church should not actively involve itself in revolutionary movements such as those represented by the Liberation Theologians or the anti-apartheid groups. Instead, he told his bishops and clergy to maintain the principles of the Church. For those clergy hoping to hear a different message, it was another bitter blow. However, the pope did refuse an invitation by the government of South Africa to visit, lest it appear that the Church supported its apartheid policies.

A HISTORIC VISIT

The pope now turned his focus closer to home: the relations between the Communists in Poland, Eastern Europe, and the Soviet Union, and the "Church of Silence," as the Catholic Church was referred to behind the Iron Curtain. Communist officials were still reeling from Lolek's election. Now they faced a formidable challenge to their authority from a pope who was going to be difficult to ignore. It was clear that Communist leaders would have to step very carefully in their dealings with him. The stakes in the game of *Ostpolitik* had risen considerably.

As early as the end of 1978, the pope had given strong hints that he would like to return to Poland for a visit, and proposed that he come in May, 1979, for the 900th anniversary of the murder of St. Stanislaw, the nation's first martyr. The Polish government, wanting to avoid any religious connection with a possible visit, asked that the pope come in August instead. Finally it appeared that a compromise was reached for a June visit. However, the pope issued an apostolic letter that, in effect, stated he would be celebrating St. Stanislaw's feast day the week he would be visiting Poland. On the surface at least, it appeared as if everyone had gotten their way. But the government, aware that the pontiff had outwitted them, was clearly nervous about the visit. For the first time in many years, the Polish people would gather in large masses and government authorities feared that an uprising could be sparked by the papal visit.

On June 2, the pope arrived in Warsaw. Over the course of the next nine days, it has been estimated that close to 10 million Poles saw him in one of the cities or towns and sanctuaries that he visited. The country was awash in red and white Polish flags and the white and yellow colors of the papacy. John Paul II's appearances drew some of the largest crowds in history. Those who could not see the pope in person watched him on television. And even though the government ordered television crews to focus only on the pope and not the huge crowds who had gathered to see him, Poles everywhere knew that the country had turned out to greet its native son. Many Poles regarded the papal visit as "our nine days of freedom."[7] People from the other eastern bloc countries were not forgotten either. The many signs beseeching the pope to "Remember Your Czech Children" led John Paul II to respond to the crowds that he had not forgotten any of the Catholics who lived in the countries of the "Silent Church."

The international press followed him everywhere he went. The pope visited his boyhood home of Wadowice and greeted old friends. Though he was barred from visiting certain areas, such as Silesia, the site of continual labor unrest, the pope would not be deterred. Everywhere he met miners and workers, he called on them to think for themselves. In his speeches and sermons to his countrymen his message came through loud and clear: the Communists were masters only if the Poles allowed it. It was a powerful statement.

Certainly one of the most poignant moments of the pope's trip was his visit to the concentration camp sites at Auschwitz and Birkenau. Even though it was not John Paul II's first visit, it was the first time a pontiff had ever come to the camps. Walking slowly along the paths of the camp, the pope passed thirty stone tablets in a variety of languages. He then knelt before three stone tablets, each of which was inscribed in Hebrew, Russian, and Polish. After praying, he spoke: "This nation which received from God Jahwe the Commandment, 'Thou Shall Not Kill,' has itself experienced killing in a particular manner.... Nobody may walk past this...in indifference."[8]

The pope then spent the last days of his visit in Kraków where he toured Jagiellonian University and met with students. He also squeezed in meetings with bishops and priests, and took time to visit the sick and infirm. He said Mass, kissed babies, and proclaimed his message of patriotism, faith, and hope. It was, by all accounts, a masterful accomplishment by one man. On his last day, he celebrated a Mass in honor of St. Stanislaw that was attended by three million persons. At the end, balloons were let into the air bearing the sign of the anti-Communist resistance movement of the 1940s. As one friend of the pope's later described it: "There was this feeling of a whole city being on fire, of sitting on a pile of powder and they were handing him the matches. And he [the pope] was saying, 'I'm going to tell you how to use this power in a different way.'"[9]

The pope's pilgrimage to Poland profoundly affected future political developments in that country. It brought millions together at rallies and open-air Masses, helped to break the barrier of fear erected by the Communist regime to forestall independent social activities, reaffirmed Christian values, and sparked anti-Communist resistance. The visit displayed the vulnerability and unpopularity of the regime and acted as a catalyst for the birth of the Solidarity free labor movement a year later. According to the pope's secretary, the papal visit "was the great moment. There was a crowd of one million people, and he told them 'You are men. You have dignity. Don't crawl on your bellies.' It was the beginning of the end of the Soviet Union."[10]

THE PILGRIM POPE

No sooner was the Pope back in Rome than he began preparations for another journey to Ireland and the United States. While in the United States, the pope visited the United Nations in New York City where he gave a speech against nuclear armaments and in favor of a more vigilant stance on the part of the superpowers to defend human rights. He also visited the White House, becoming the first pope ever to do so. From there, John Paul II went on to Philadelphia and Chicago, where he was welcomed by large, enthusiastic crowds. But his speeches did not always endear him to Americans. If John Paul II was openly critical of the totalitarian governments that abused human rights, he was no more enamored of what he viewed as the selfish and egotistical abuse of personal freedom that was a part of capitalist society. During his United States visit, the pope denounced rampant materialism and superficial pleasure-seeking as another violation of personal dignity and spiritual health.

In addressing a group of nuns in Washington, D.C., John Paul II made clear his views on the role of women in the church. Welcoming him on behalf of the group was Sister Theresa Kane, Superior of the Sisters of Mercy and head of the Leadership Conference of Religious Women, a kind of union for nuns. Sister Kane was also a feminist who complained to the pope about the "intense suffering and pain" that women of the Church endured. She then asked John Paul II if it wasn't time for the

Catholic Church to include women "in all the ministries of the Church," especially the priesthood.[11]

Replying firmly but politely, the pope reminded the group that the Virgin Mary was the model for women, stating, "Without herself being inserted into the hierarchy...of the Church, [she] made all hierarchy possible because she gave to the world the shepherd and bishop of our souls."[12] Many in the room found the pope's remark off-putting and believed him to be telling women that they should be content to serve the Church in an auxiliary role. While the pope handled the situation with tact, privately, he was very angry with Kane and her confrontational manner. Upon his return to Rome he ordered that the Mothers General of the major orders of nuns send an admonishing note to Kane about her behavior. But the issue was far from over, and the pope never really understood the discontent that many Catholic women felt toward the Church.

While in the United States, the pope also reminded American Catholics of the Church's stance on birth control. Speaking before a crowd attending an open-air Mass on the Washington Mall, the pope stated that:

> Decisions about the number of children [to have] and the sacrifices to be made for them must not be taken only with a view to...comfort.... It is certainly less serious to deny...children certain comforts or material advantages than to deprive them of brothers and sisters who could help them to grow in humanity.[13]

At the same time, he told priests at Washington's Catholic University of American that it was their responsibility to safeguard the Church's teachings, which meant accepting them without question, while stressing that "freedom of investigation" was necessary in teaching.[14] It was a decidedly contradictory message with regard to the Church's teachings, and the first of many that the Pope was accused of sending. The pope also stressed the tenets of his own book of philosophy, *The Acting Person* (the english translation of his 1969 work Person and Act), which stated that actions—not thoughts or statements—define what a person stands for. John Paul clearly took an activist approach to his papacy, rather than passively stating beliefs and principles from within the Vatican.

In November, the pope departed Rome for Turkey to meet with the head of the Eastern Orthodox Church in an attempt to reconcile differences between the two major Christian denominations in the world. The meetings accomplished little. The Turkish trip marked the establishment

of a pattern in John Paul II's papacy. Although willing to resolve outstanding differences with other faiths, the pope rarely made discernable
progress.

When the pope arrived home from Turkey, new problems awaited him.
Some Vatican officials said privately that the new pope was traveling too
much, giving a triumphant face to Catholicism, when he should have
been concentrating on rebuilding the Church from behind his desk, in
the Vatican. When asked about this criticism, John Paul responded, "Yes,
I agree! I am traveling too much. But sometimes it is necessary to do
something of what is too much!"[15] Even his vacations—skiing and
hiking—amplified his activist image, revealing an athleticism unprecedented in the modern papacy.

Besides facing internal squabbling over his travel, the pope also had to
deal with the growing problem of dissent among Catholic scholars and
theologians. In 1986, the Vatican told Father Charles Curran, a professor
at the Catholic University in Washington, D.C., that he was no longer
suitable to teach theology, based on his public opposition to *Humanae
Vitae*. In 1988, when French Archbishop Marcel Lefebvre rejected Vatican II reforms and began ordaining his own priests and bishops, the pope
excommunicated the ultraconservative cleric. Then, in December of
1989, Swiss theologian Hans Küng learned that his license to teach theology had been revoked. Küng had questioned the doctrine of papal infallibility, a doctrine in place since 1870, that declared the pope infallible,
that is, incapable of error, when pronouncing on matters of Catholic faith
and morals. Küng's challenge made worldwide headlines, and the pope's
censure triggered protests from a number of episcopates. But the pope refused to lift the sanctions against Küng. A year later, in 1990, the pope
also punished Father Jacques Pohier for questioning the resurrection of
Christ, one of the central tenets of all Christian faiths.

In addition to Curran, Lefebvre, Küng, and Pohier, John Paul II singled
out other, less notable figures for punishment. He cracked down on priests
who were politically active, particularly those who held public office.
While directing most of his wrath toward Latin American clergy who followed Liberation Theology, John Paul II reminded one North American
priest of his duties and his place. The liberal Massachusetts cleric Father
Robert Drinan, who was elected state representative to Congress, was
forced to resign his office. In ordering all priests to cease participating in
secular party politics, the pope did not wish to weaken Catholicism's political impact but to unify the church and strengthen its moral authority.
He wanted Catholic social doctrine to be delivered with the singular au-

thority of Rome, not altered or reinterpreted by cleric politicians, whose priestly office ought to supersede their secular ambitions.

THE BEGINNING OF A NEW DECADE

The 1980s was the zenith of Pope John Paul II's papacy. He enjoyed enormous diplomatic successes and made great strides for the Church. But the 1980s was also a period in which he suffered tragedy, grief, and danger. While affairs in Poland occupied a great deal of his time, he also understood the importance of being accessible to Catholics all over the world. Modern technology, whether jet planes, television cameras, satellite television, or computers, made it possible for him to reach large numbers of people. By these means, the pope delivered the Catholic message, recruiting new followers to the Church and building bridges between the Church and its present members.

During his travels over the next decade, John Paul singled out the Soviet Union with his messages of religious freedom, national independence, and human rights. He proved a constant irritant to the Kremlin with his declarations that all of Europe should be reunited through its common Christian heritage. In 1981, he led an international colloquium entitled, "The Common Christian Roots of the European Nations." But none of these activities would have made any difference if were not for the personal charisma of the pope.

John Paul II was an imaginative pontiff. Yet, he was also completely unaware of how to deal with the new generation of Catholics and lacked a clear comprehension of the problems facing both the industrial countries of the West and the poor countries of the Third World. Although John Paul II could be flexible, he had already shown an iron will that refused to bend or compromise. These contradictory traits continued to define his papacy in the years to come.

A COUNTRY IN CRISIS

A new crisis erupted in Poland during John Paul II's trip to Brazil. It came near the end of a very hectic travel schedule that took the pontiff to three continents and nine countries. His first stop was a 10-day tour of Africa beginning in May, visiting Zaire, Congo, Kenya, Ghana, Upper Volta, and the Ivory Coast. The visit was particularly significant to John Paul II for Africa symbolized the last frontier of Roman Catholicism and was a region the pope returned to more than any other nation or continent in his travels. Here the Church was competing for followers in a land that still practiced the traditional African religions, as well as Islam and Protestantism. But once again, the Church's resistance to change, acculturation, or the blending of African and Christian traditions proved an ongoing obstacle to gaining Catholic converts.

From Africa, John Paul II visited France for four days, the first pope to do so since 1814. While there, he spoke to gatherings of young people and addressed UNESCO on the importance of preserving cultures and civilizations. Then, on June 30, the pope left for Brazil, the first time ever a pope had visited that country.

Meanwhile, on July 1, 1980, the Polish government announced a new series of price increases on food, another sign of the rapidly deteriorating economic and social situation. In protest, strikes broke out throughout the country, beginning in Lublin. By July 16, the agitation had spread to the railroad system in Lublin. As grave as the situation was, no one, from the government to the pope to the workers themselves, had any idea of what was about to take place.

The Lublin railway strike was of concern to Moscow as Soviet troops, stationed in East Germany, relied on that railroad link for supplies and food. By July 27, with order seemingly restored, a nervous President Gierek flew to Moscow to reassure authorities that all was well. It wasn't. The strikes continued to spread. Spontaneous work stoppages took place in many of the major industrial centers and there was a mood of rebellion throughout Poland. The pope, now back in Rome, watched with interest as events unfolded, but did nothing.

Then on August 14, 1980, workers at the Lenin Shipyard in Gdańsk came forward with a new demand: the creation of independent labor unions that would exist along with the government-controlled unions. Led by an unemployed electrician, Lech Walesa, the workers threatened not to leave the premises until their demands were met. The situation was reaching a crisis point and government authorities were unsure what to do next. The situation was exacerbated by the heavily Catholic overtones of the workers' actions; they erected a large wooden cross in front of the shipyard entrance, and hung papal flags and portraits of the pope on the gates. Other shipyards joined in the work stoppage and in those critical days, a new political movement was born: Solidarity. While the pope had not sanctioned the move by the workers, it was as if he had extended his protection to them. Government officials knew they must proceed most carefully or risk having the pope intervene.

The Lenin Shipyard strike emerged as a powerful international event as the world watched to see what would happen next. The Polish government, not willing to risk another violent confrontation, also waited. On Monday, August 16, the leaders of Solidarity presented a list of demands. Negotiations with the government went on for the rest of the month. In the meantime, Soviet Premier Leonid Brezhnev made it clear that the situation in Poland needed to be resolved quickly, as the Soviets feared the possible collapse of the entire system. Through all of this, John Paul II remained in contact with Cardinal Wyszyński, but publicly stayed silent. He also opened up discussions with Brezhnev, assuring him in a letter that the unrest would not threaten the Soviet Union. At the same time, however, he began sending secret correspondence to the members of Solidarity.

By autumn, the Polish government agreed to Solidarity's demand for independent labor unions, which were formally organized on September 22, 1980, when delegates of 36 regional trade unions met in Gdańsk and united under the name Solidarnos. Lech Walesa was elected chairman of Solidarity. A separate agricultural union composed of private farmers, named Rural Solidarity, was founded in Warsaw on December 14, 1980. By early 1981, Solidarity had a membership of about 10 million and represented most of the workforce of Poland.

The forming of Solidarity marked the first time that a Communist regime had abandoned its monopoly on power over the working class; it was a stirring signal for future political change and sent shock waves throughout the communist and free world. Officials at the Kremlin were less than pleased, and while there was talk of a possible invasion to stop Solidarity from gaining any more ground, by mid-December, government officials decided against it. The pope, while keeping in contact with the Kremlin, prepared to leave on another trip, this time to West Germany in November. By early December, Solidarity spokesmen announced that workers were back on the job. Now a new triumvirate had emerged in Poland: the government, the Church, and Solidarity. As a sign of the organization's stature, in January, 1981, the pope greeted a Solidarity delegation led by Lech Walesa at the Vatican.

By February, the pope was off again, this time to visit Japan and the Philippines. While in Japan, John Paul II visited Nagasaki and Hiroshima. His Japanese hosts were pleased when the pope, in his prepared remarks, spoke in Japanese and showed a deep interest and respect for their culture.

ASSASSINATION ATTEMPT

On May 13, 1981, the unthinkable happened. Twenty-three-year-old Turkish terrorist Mehmet Ali Agca fired a large Browning handgun at the pope's car as it moved through St. Peter's Square, which was filled with tourists and spectators. The bullet hit the pope in the abdomen, shattering the colon and small intestine, but just missing the central aorta. As Agca tried to run away screaming, "Not me! Not me!" he was stopped by a nun, Sister Letizia, who, grabbing onto the assassin's arm yelled, "Yes you!" while the police came.[16]

The pope's condition was critical for the next five hours as surgeons operated to repair the damage. Thanks to his excellent physical condition, his recovery was relatively speedy, though at one point he almost died from an infection that was caused by the emergency blood transfusion he had received. Four days after he was shot, the pope publicly forgave Agca. Four months later, the pope made his first public appearance in St. Peter's Square.

It soon came to light that Agca had not acted alone as was thought. It was believed the attempted assassination plot was conceived by Communist authorities in Bulgaria and the Soviet Union, though documents found in the secret archives after the collapse of the Soviet Union revealed little. Even today, the assassination attempt on the pope remains a great mystery. Some believe that a conspiracy existed, particularly given the situation in Poland and Eastern Europe during the early 1980s. To kill the pope would have been a great blow to the Polish people and to Solidarity.

In 1983, John Paul II visited Agca in prison where he told Agca he forgave him for his actions, leaving the stunned Agca asking him, "How is it that I could not kill you?"[17] Officials in the Vatican also believe that by forgiving his assailant, the pope was telling the Soviet Union that he had no desire to learn any more. For the pope, anything that might endanger the political situation in Poland and world peace was not worth pursuing.

A COUNTRY ENDANGERED

In September of 1981, the pope published his *Laborem Exercens*, "On Human Work," which dealt with the rights of workers, his first encyclical to address that topic. However, in Poland, workers were stepping up their demands, creating an increasingly tense situation. Throughout 1981, the Polish government, now led by General Wojciech Jaruzelski, was confronted by a series of controlled strikes to back up workers' appeals for economic reforms, free elections, and the involvement of trade unions in decision making at the highest levels. Solidarity's positions hardened as the moderate Walesa came under pressure by more militant unionists.

Jaruzelski's government, meanwhile, was subjected to severe pressure from the Soviet Union to suppress Solidarity.

On December 13, 1981, Jaruzelski imposed martial law on Poland in a bid to crush the Solidarity movement. Solidarity was declared illegal, and its leaders were arrested. Jaruzelski's reasons were simple: by imposing martial law, he hoped to avoid outside interference from the Soviets and to prevent a civil war among his own people. The pope's reaction to the crisis was swift. In an address to Polish pilgrims given that same day, the pope asked for prayers for the people of Poland, and hoped that no blood would be shed. The union was formally dissolved by the Sejm (the Polish Parliament) on October 8, 1982, but it nevertheless continued as an underground organization, which still received secret communications from the pope.

A SEEMING CONTRADICTION

By this time, the Polish government and the Church had achieved some measure of cordial relations, even though the Church was a staunch supporter of Solidarity. Still, both parties were negotiating the possibility of a return trip to Poland by the pope in 1982. That same year, Father Jerzy Popieluszko began joining sit-ins and speaking out against the regime. Poles flocked to his church because of his radical politics and the pope encouraged his work by sending him a crucifix. It was not long before Father Popieluszko became such a threat that the Communists had him murdered.

Meanwhile, in South America, John Paul II continued to speak out against priestly involvement in politics, a seemingly contradictory position given his support for Solidarity. According to one scholar, the pope "is a Pole [and] he does not compromise with secular authority. The whole history of Polish Catholicism, of Polish romantic nationalism, of Polish idealism in all its political and secular forms is a history of non-compromise."[18] Keeping close track of developments in Poland did not prevent the pope from making travel plans as well as engaging in some international relations of his own. Two of the planned trips that year to Great Britain and Argentina involved countries that were about to go to war against each other over control of the Falkland Islands, located off the Argentine coast. While his advisors strongly suggested he postpone both trips, the pope came up with another idea: celebrating a "Reconciliation Mass" with the English and Argentine cardinals. The service was a success and while it did not stop war from breaking out, the pope's brilliant diplomatic move allowed him to visit both nations without repercussions. When, however, he did visit Argentina in 1982, he decried the Falklands war. Catholic priests and nuns, by contrast, expressed their support for it by waving banners that read, "Holy Father bless our war."

In 1983, John Paul II traveled to Central America where Catholic clerics held a number of positions in the left-wing government. He publicly scolded Ernesto Cardenal, a Trappist monk and Nicaraguan Minister of Culture. In private, the pope negotiated the excommunication of Miguel D'Escoto, a Jesuit who had joined Nicaragua's communist Sandinista government with permission from his order. In 1984, the Brazilian Franciscan Leonardo Boff, a brilliant liberation theologian, was summoned to the Vatican to answer for his latest book. In it, he used Marxist language to critique the Church and analyze its mission. In the end, like other scholars who had criticized the Church, he was silenced, forbidden from speaking or publishing his work.

A CURIOUS GROUP

Some papal biographers have suggested that during this period the pope forged an alliance of sorts with U.S. President Ronald Reagan to bring about the collapse of communism. While the two did meet in 1982 at the Vatican, there never was a formal union or plan on how to deal with the Soviets. Undoubtedly, the president and pope did talk of the situation in Poland and the Soviet Union, but the visible result of that conference was the re-establishment of diplomatic ties between the two countries, which had been severed in 1867. The United States government also provided the pope with private briefings on world affairs through the former CIA director, Lieutenant General Vernon Walters. The Vatican, in turn, volunteered to mediate between NATO and the Soviet Union to negotiate an agreement on halting deployment of nuclear weapons in Europe.

But the man with whom the pope continued to correspond the most throughout this period was General Jaruzelski. When Jaruzelski explained to John Paul II his reasons for imposing martial law, the pope was said to have understood and agreed that the general's policy was the wisest course of action. While the pope's relationships with Lech Walesa and later Soviet Premier Mikhail Gorbachev were forged in haste, the relationship with Jaruzelski was much subtler and closer.

By November 1982, Soviet Premier Leonid Brezhnev was dead. In Warsaw, General Jaruzelski announced an end to the martial law, and many of the Solidarity leaders, including Lech Walesa, were released from jail. In the meantime, plans for the pope's proposed visit to Poland to take place in 1983 went ahead after the Communist party's Central Committee concluded that the visit posed no risk to the Soviet presence in Poland.

The Pope's 1983 visit to his homeland, while important, was more subdued than his triumphant return in 1979. For one thing, the visit was much shorter, lasting only a week. During his trip, the pope visited Warsaw where he met with General Jaruzelski. He also had a brief meeting with Walesa. In between, he traveled and celebrated Mass. Although concerned about the current state of Polish affairs, the pope continued to watch developments with a cautious eye, and continued to keep in close contact with Jaruzelski.

The pope also kept up with Church affairs. In his quest to promote diversity within the Catholic Church, the pope appointed 27 new cardinals in 1983. In making his choices, the pope strove to find men of keen intellect, rather than men who would conform to his views. His selections represented regions from all over the world, but particularly Eastern Europe, Africa, Latin America, and Asia. He also appointed an African Cardinal Gantin of Benin as prefect of the Congregation of Bishops, one of the top positions in the Vatican. It was the first time an African had ever been appointed to such a high Church office.

A NEW SOVIET LEADER

In March of 1985, a new Soviet premier was elected. Mikhail Gorbachev signaled a new era in Soviet history, one that had dramatic repercussions by the end of the decade. Under Gorbachev, a restructuring or *perestróika* of Soviet policies was underway. In Poland, meanwhile, Jaruzelski, in studying the results of a survey, found that the majority of Poles identified themselves as believers in the Church and participated regularly in religious services. These survey results, while disappointing, were no surprise to the Polish government. It was clear to them that religion, the Catholic Church, and most of all the pope, were a permanent part of Polish life.

Jaruzelski then decided to partner with the Catholic Church in preparation for what appeared to be a transition from Communist rule to a free government. The situation in Poland was helped along a year later by Gorbachev's announcement that the Soviet bloc countries were entitled to choose their own way of governing and to decide their own fate. It was a momentous and exhilarating proposition. That same year, 1985, Jaruzelski met with the pope. Among their topics of discussion was another proposed visit by the pope to Poland in 1987. It was a warm visit; to the pope, Jaruzelski had shown himself to be a man of his word. As he had promised, he had lifted martial law, released political prisoners, and lessened the day-to-day restrictions on the Polish people. The pope also realized that the events taking place in Poland were not isolated and would reverberate powerfully throughout Europe and the world. Jaruzelski would also be instrumental in bringing the pope and Gorbachev together.

A NEW POLAND—A NEW BEGINNING

The pope's third visit to Poland in June, 1987, still evoked great enthusiasm among the Poles, as the country edged closer to independence. The Polish government made no attempt to stop the pope from visiting once-restricted places and backed off when John Paul II requested a meeting with Walesa. The pope and the general also met twice, conferring on the current state of affairs, with Jaruzelski promising that Church and party representatives would meet on a regular basis.

By the next year, events moved ahead rapidly. Gorbachev visited Poland in July, receiving a warm reception, a first for a Soviet premier. Yet, a new wave of strikes and labor unrest spread across Poland. Prominent among the strikers' demands was government recognition of Solidarity. General Jaruzelski realized he had little choice but to lay the foundation for a new Polish government.

In April of 1989, the government agreed to legalize Solidarity and allow it to participate in free elections to a bicameral Polish parliament. The government also established diplomatic ties with the Vatican, formalizing a relationship that had in effect been going on since the pope took office in 1979. In the elections held in June, candidates endorsed by Solidarity won 99 of 100 seats in the newly formed Senate and all 161 of the contested seats in the Sejm, or lower house. In August, Solidarity agreed to form a coalition government, and a longtime Solidarity adviser, Tadeusz Mazowiecki became the first non-Communist premier to govern Poland since the late 1940s. In December of 1990, Walesa was elected president of Poland.

In the midst of these historic events, Gorbachev visited with Pope John Paul in December 1989. For 20 minutes the two men chatted about the current state of affairs, and Gorbachev suggested that perhaps it was time for the Soviet Union and the Vatican to establish diplomatic ties, a proposal that came to fruition in 1990. Gorbachev also indicated to the pope that he was prepared to lift the long-standing restrictions on religious and other freedoms throughout Eastern Europe. In return, Gorbachev hoped to have the Church's support for *perestroika*. The meeting marked the beginning of a special friendship between the two men, one that continued long after Gorbachev was ousted from office in 1991.

The 1980s brought a number of personal triumphs for the pope. His world travels now were legendary; since 1980 he had visited Poland twice, Latin America four times, Asia and Africa twice, and Canada once. He also visited six Western European countries, including Germany and France. He had written a number of encyclicals and preached to hundreds of thousands of persons. He had courted controversy and showed himself capable of earnest and sometimes angry debate. He had survived an assassination attempt.

These were all great accomplishments, but for John Paul II, being able to watch his fellow Poles participate in the first free elections since 1938 was something very special. There is a general consensus that these historic events would not have happened without the pope.

NOTES

1. Tad Szulc, *Pope John Paul II: The Biography* (New York: Scribner, 1995), p. 282.

2. Ibid., p. 286.

3. Robert Andreas, ed., *Pope John Paul II: A Tribute* (Boston: Bulfinch Press, 1999), p. 83.

4. Ibid.

5. Carl Bernstein and Marco Politi, *His Holiness: John Paul II and the Hidden History of Our Time* (New York: Doubleday, 1996), p. 183.

6. Ibid.

7. Szulc, p. 303.

8. Ibid., p. 306.

9. Jonathan Kwitney, *Man of the Century: The Life and Times of Pope John Paul II* (New York: Henry Holt, 1997), p. 329.

10. "The Papal Years: Charisma and Restoration," accessed December 4, 2001, located at: http://www.cnn.com/SPECIALS/1999/pope/bio/papal/index.html.

11. Kwitney, p. 340.

12. Ibid.

13. Ibid.

14. Ibid.

15. Ibid.

16. Andreas, p. 89.

17. "The Papal Years: Charisma and Restoration."

18. Jane Barnes, "Frontline: The Millennial Pope," accessed June 10, 2002, located at: http://www.pbs.org/wgbh/pages/frontline/shows/pope/etc/bio2.html.

Chapter 10

MAN OF THE YEAR—MAN OF THE CENTURY

Entering the second decade of his papacy, Pope John Paul II began show-ing signs of increasing frustration. The 1980s had been characterized by his preoccupation with the political changes in Poland and Eastern Eu-rope. During the 1980s, the pope had not softened his message, using every opportunity to speak about the Church's teachings and to impose discipline on the faithful. But the pope was also showing his feelings; on occasion audiences saw an angry pope, a rare sight just a few years earlier. There was still the problem of a growing dissent within the Church, mak-ing it harder for the pope to achieve his goal of a united Roman Catholic Church. It was also becoming clear that Catholics, particularly those in the West, were not heeding the pope's advice and messages.

In the 1990s the pope took an even harder stance on hot button issues such as birth control, abortion, and the role of women in the Church, while continuing to play an important role in world events and weigh in on issues and controversies around the world. Already in June of 1990, the Vatican ordered Catholic theologians to stop quarreling with the Church publicly; if they had problems with certain Catholic doctrines, they were not, under any circumstances, to air their disagreements in public. Disobeying this order would earn them the same fate as others who had defied the pope and Church teachings.

In the midst of this ongoing internal squabble, there were several other concerns facing the pope. The Church was continuing to lose ground among its followers and many clergy feared that the institution was losing its moral, political, and social relevance. Adding to the problem was the refusal of some world leaders to listen to the pope. When the pope pleaded with U.S. President George Bush to negotiate a last-minute retreat from Kuwait in 1990, the president listened, but then ignored the pope, whom he viewed as nothing more than a second-rate and unreliable ally. The pope received another bitter jolt when the government of Israel refused to allow the Vatican to participate in a conference in Madrid, which would hopefully lead to future talks with the Palestinians. And in the most bitter irony of all, with the fall of the Soviet Union in 1991, the pope and the Church suffered a serious erosion of power and influence in Russia. As depressing as that seemed, there was something even more troubling awaiting the pope on his next trip to Poland.

A DISAPPOINTING HOMECOMING

Arriving in Warsaw on June 1, 1991, the pope was welcomed by President Lech Walesa, who hailed him as a modern-day Moses who had led his people to the Promised Land. But to the pope's dismay, when he now spoke or preached, the people did not appear as interested as they once were. Although Poles were willing to be led, it was no longer by the Church. Communism had fallen in Poland, but John Paul II was soon to be bitterly disappointed by his countrymen's response to freedom.

Poland had changed, and in the pope's eyes, not for the better. Where he had once hoped that his homeland would lead the world in restoring spiritual values, he saw now that his countrymen embraced not the tenets of the Church but of Western capitalism and materialism, and all that they symbolized: consumerism, licentiousness, and to the pope's horror, legalized abortion. The Poles no longer wished for the Church to interfere in their private lives, viewing the institution with the same distrust with which they once had regarded the Communists.

For eight days, the pope worked his way across Poland, delivering sermon after sermon. Now Poles saw an angry, fierce, and defiant pope, emphasizing the dangers of modern life. He opposed the proposed Polish Constitution, which would separate Church and State, stating that "The principle of absolutely refusing to admit the dimension of the holy into social or governmental life means introducing atheism into state and society."[1]

The pope also spoke out against adultery and divorce and attacked the media for distorting the truth about the Catholic church. He explained that contrary to public opinion, the Church was not out to regulate society, but merely to guide it, and that the current economic crisis of the nation was moving hand in hand with an ethical one. He preached against Poland fully embracing the culture of the West. "We don't need to 'enter' Europe," he told an audience in the city of Wloclawek, "because we helped to create it in the first place; and we went to more trouble doing it than those who claim a monopoly on Europeanism." His speeches were a mixture of prepared remarks and impromptu comments. In attacking utilitarianism and the current notions of sexuality in Western Europe and the United States, the pope stated, "As the bishop of Rome, I protest against the way they wish to reduce the concept of Europe," and condemned "the whole civilization of desire and pleasure which is now lording over us." He then regained his composure and said to his audience, "Pardon my burning words. But I had to say them."[2]

To his dismay, he found many Poles disregarding his advice. Now people saw no contradiction in calling themselves Catholic and opposing a ban on abortion. For the first time, the pope was encountering hostility among his fellow Poles. It was a shocking and bitter experience for him. Poles who had once cheered for him were now irritated. In the midst of a terrible economic crisis, which had left close to 2,000,000 persons unemployed, people felt the pope was living in a dreamworld. Particularly angry with him were mothers; already feeling the hardship of caring for children, they did not want to be forced to bring more mouths to feed into the world. He was further disappointed when he learned that some of the Polish clergy, as well as several leading government officials, supported lifting the ban on abortion.

John Paul II returned to Rome disheartened and angry. He believed that the Church deserved better treatment, considering the role it had played in the collapse of communism. He became deeply troubled over the future and told the Polish bishops before he left, "Earlier, the Church received wide-spread recognition even from lay circles. But in the present-day situation there is no counting on such recognition. Instead we have to be ready for criticism and perhaps something worse."[3] But others saw the pope's visit differently. Ewa Kulik had been one of those entrusted to carry messages from the pope to Solidarity members. She described the pope as a man who had lost touch with his country. We had so many problems. Instead of even talking about them, he talked about these things we were sick and tired of—abortion. Instead of trying to understand us and teach us he was wagging his finger: "Everything that comes from the West is corrupt—liberalism, capitalism, pornography."[4]

Meanwhile, as the military dictators fell and civil wars ebbed in Latin America, the base communities that were at the heart of Liberation Theology survived. They fostered the sort of social fabric the pope approved of: communal solidarity built around the church. It was a bitter irony for John Paul II.

THE CULTURE OF MATERIALISM

During the 1990s, one of the pope's primary targets was consumerism, particularly the rampant materialism that John Paul II viewed as a "kind of virus...that is spreading from West to East."[5] As the decade wore on, the pope stepped up his crusade against materialism and Western culture. With increasing forthrightness, he came to view many of the founders of modern Western thought, including Austrian psychoanalyst Sigmund Freud, German philosopher Frederich Nietzsche, and many of the Enlightenment thinkers, as profoundly anti-Christian.

John Paul II also saw modern history for the last three centuries as a perpetual struggle to eliminate all that is Christian. What the pope feared most was that in celebrating the idea of man as a complete being, humanity was cutting itself off from its moral compass, particularly the teachings of the Church. This attitude proved costly for the pope, as many Catholics and potential converts rejected what they saw as a Church unwilling to engage in dialogue with the modern world.

A HINDERED CRUSADE

Increasingly the pope's deeply conservative views hampered his efforts. It seemed that everywhere he turned, John Paul II was facing a growing schism within the Church from both clergy and laity. In Holland, growing numbers of bishops were openly questioning papal infallibility and wanted limits put on the power of the papacy. Yet, the pope did not let up on what he believed were crucial issues of Catholic unity. Instead of Dutch candidates for the priesthood attending college, the pope ordered them to attend seminaries to receive the proper training. There were also disagreements with the pope over issues such as homosexuality (which he considered deviant and sinful), birth control, divorce (including the pope's refusal to allow divorced persons to receive communion), abortion, women priests, and cooperation with Protestant churches. The pope and his spokesmen argued that the Dutch clergy were going far beyond what the Vatican II reforms had ever intended and that they needed to return to the mainstream of Catholic thought.

American Catholics were mounting their own campaign against the pope, even going so far as to buy a full-page ad in the *New York Times* to advocate diversity of opinion within the Church. Many of the priests and nuns who initially signed the open letter to the pope later retracted or backed away from the statement, fearing censure from the Vatican. Adding more ill will toward the pope was the withdrawal of the Vatican imprimatur from the American adult catechism, *Christ Among Us*. The rejection of this popular book, which had sold 1.6 million copies in sixteen years, was a shock to the Catholic publisher, Paulist Press, as well as the Catholic community in the United States. According to the Vatican, the book's passages on saints, divorce, masturbation, homosexuality, contraception, and Vatican II, were so misleading or wrong that even major rewriting would not solve the problems. Another Catholic publisher, Crossroad Press, was ordered to withdraw publication of the book *Challenge to Love: Gay and Lesbian Catholics in the Church*, because the Vatican found the subject objectionable.

While John Paul II's defenders stated that by speaking out on these and other controversial topics, the pope was merely trying to have the Church speak with a unified voice, not limit the exchange of ideas. Whatever it took to maintain unity within the Church, the pope believed, would be worth the cost, for Catholicism had to remain the "uncompromised beacon of truth."[6] In reality, the pope was not only paying a high price to preserve unity, but in some cases was courting the very divisiveness he sought to avoid.

Just as John Paul II's efforts to better communicate within the Church often failed, so too did his attempts to improve relations with other faiths. To reconcile the Catholic Church and the Episcopal Churches, the pope, while open to possible reunification of the two faiths, resisted any suggestion that women ought to enter the priesthood, a practice the Episcopal Church had already adopted. Even though talks continued, it soon became apparent that little would come of the discussions.

Within his own Church, the pope faced a growing number of Catholics who wished to see the role of women expanded. A *Time* magazine/CNN poll taken in 1992 showed that two thirds of Catholics thought women should be in the priesthood. But it soon became clear that the Church was not interested in pursuing the matter, and in fact, positively resisted such initiatives. In 1992, American bishops finally shelved a pastoral letter that had been in the works for nine years that was to address the role and place of women in the Church and society. While some clergy flatly dismissed the notion of women priests, others wanted to keep the door open for further study and debate.

Then there was the issue of birth control. Polls in Europe and North America showed that clear majorities wished the Church to relax its stand on birth control and abortion and that many Catholic women rejected the Church's teachings on contraception, divorce, and celibacy outright. Even more troubling were the results taken from the same poll that showed only 14 percent of American Catholics felt bound to the Vatican's moral teachings; the majority believed the Church had no business interfering with their private lives. The pope, while unhappy with what he was seeing, did not waver in his beliefs, but continued to urge Catholics around the world to comply with Church teachings.

Another troubling issue facing the Church during the 1990s was the priesthood. Since 1979, when John Paul II was elected to the papacy, the number of Roman Catholics in the world had increased 19 percent. However, the number of priests had dropped almost 4 percent. While many bishops were alarmed at the decreasing numbers of vocations, the pope was not. John Paul II believed it was more important to have men of "quality," that is, intellect, dedication, and deep faith, as priests. He also believed that with time, these types of men would draw others into the priesthood. Lowering standards in order to increase the number of priests would only create inferior priests, and possibly drive away more desirable candidates. The pope also pointed out that the decline was occurring only in Europe and North America; Third World ordinations were on the increase.

The issue of declining numbers also brought up the troublesome subject of priestly celibacy. When some bishops suggested to the pope that celibacy was an unattractive and unattainable expectation, the pope dismissed their concerns. Some bishops also suggested that perhaps it might be necessary to ordain older men or married men in order to overcome the shortage of priests. The pope refused these alternatives, too, stating that "calling upon the *viri probati*" [men of tested faith] was systematic propaganda hostile to priestly celibacy."[7] John Paul II believed that priestly celibacy was a symbol of a life committed completely to God and God's Church, and that Catholics needed such examples in their lives.

The pope had also cracked down on the Vatican policy of granting resignations to priests who wished to leave their vocation. Compared to Paul VI, who had granted 31,324 resignations out of 32,357 applications, and the 200 granted by John Paul I during his brief tenure in office, John Paul II refused to let priests have an easy out. Comparing the unreliability of priests to sustain their vocation to the increasingly easy manner of ending marriages, the pope wrote:

> It is a matter here of keeping one's word to Christ and the Church.... Difficulties, temptation do not spare the priest any more than they spare any other Christian.... Our brothers and sisters joined by the marriage bond have the right to expect from us...the [same] witness of fidelity.[8]

One other area of contention between the pope and his cardinals was the canonization of saints. In his first 10 years as pope, John Paul II beatified (added the title "blessed") 123 potential candidates for sainthood, almost double the number of all previous twentieth-century popes. He had also canonized more saints than ever with the exception of Pope Pius XII. Compared to his predecessors, John Paul II made a point of canonizing local "heroes" as a way of drawing people closer to the Church. And in more than a few cases, the pope chose to make political statements when commemorating these individuals. One such instance occurred in Spain. When the new Socialist Spanish government removed religious classes from public schools and legalized abortion, the pope resumed the sainthood process for those Catholics who died fighting for Fascist General Francisco Franco's troops during the Spanish Civil War of the 1930s. Many Spaniards were incensed at the pope's actions.

Besides creating a crowded Church calendar, the pope, some Church officials believed, was canonizing too many saints. Cardinal Joseph Ratzinger, the head of the Congregation for the Doctrine of the Faith, and one of the pope's most trusted advisors and confidantes, stated that the pope was selecting candidates "who perhaps mean something to a certain group of people, but do not mean a great deal to the multitude of believers."[9] Ratzinger's comments meant little to the pope, who as of 2000 had canonized more than 280 saints and beatified 760 others, in addition to relaxing some of the restrictions in the lengthy process of granting sainthood.

It was becoming increasingly clear that many Catholics throughout the world regarded the pope as a crusty old curmudgeon who was no longer useful. But the pope refused to be ignored. He continued his traveling, visiting Africa where he spent time in many Moslem countries. In his talks, he discussed the shared traits between Catholicism and the traditional African religions. On his return trip to Africa, the pope told reporters:

> Sometimes the question is asked, "Why does the pope always go back to Africa?" Sometimes perhaps, we Westerners, whose lives are based so much on scientific and technological process, distance ourselves from values [that are] primitive, yes, but fundamental. Try to reflect a little on this.[10]

THE POPE AND THE YOUNG

One of the highlights of John Paul II's papacy has been the World Youth Day festivals. The annual get-togethers began in Rome in 1984, when the pope wished to do more in promoting the Church's teachings among young people. Since that time, World Youth Day festivals have been held all over the world. The largest was in 1995, when approximately 4,000,000 young persons aged 16 to 24, representing as many as 107 nations, met in the Philippines. Young Catholics have carried a wooden cross around the world going from festival to festival. Entrusted to them by the pope, the cross has reportedly traveled by airplane, truck, boat, and even dog sled to its next destination.

World Youth Day combines a variety of spiritual, cultural, and charitable events. A World Youth Day choir always performs and many of the young visitors help out at food banks, hospitals, and environmental projects around the festival's location. The high point of World Youth Day is the celebration of Mass by the pope. The gatherings are among the pope's favorites; illness or injury has never kept the pope from attending a World Youth Day. Despite the commercialism of the event, where vendors hawk styrofoam pope hats and beer known as "ale mary" is sold, the pope always appears to draw energy from the teenagers and young adults who come to see and listen to him. About the World Youth Day gatherings, the pope has written, "It is not true that the Pope brings the young from one end of the world to the other. It is they who bring him. Even though he is getting older, they urge him to be young, they do not permit him to forget his experience, his discovery of youth, and its great importance for the life of every man."[11]

One of John Paul II's most memorable moments was at the 1993 World Youth Day held in Denver, Colorado, at which he participated in a nationally televised exchange with the new American president, Bill Clinton. Knowing that the president supported abortion rights, the pope then asked Clinton to "defend life" if the president really wanted to promote "justice for all and true freedom." John Paul II also wondered aloud on camera whether the Americans who came to see him were really interested in what he had to say.[12]

VERITATIS SPLENDOR

In 1993, the pope published what many theologians believe to be his masterpiece: the encyclical *Veritatis Splendor* or "The Splendor of Truth." More religious than political, *Veritatis Splendor*, which took six years to write, dwells heavily on a positive theme: namely, "that once moral imperatives are recognized as objective, real and permanent, a person can then move confidently towards...them—cheerfully accepting even martyrdom if necessary."[13]

Veritatis Splendor is divided into three chapters. In the first, the pope distinguishes negative and positive morality. For instance, the Ten Commandments are mainly prohibitions: don't kill, don't covet or steal, don't defame or blaspheme. The importance of these rules, according to the pope, is that they "express forcefully the urgent need to protect human life, the communion of persons in marriage, private property, truthfulness and people's good names." At the very least, without obeying these commands, "genuine love for God is not possible." Those who strive for the maximum find these laws liberating. By contrast, according to John Paul II, those individuals who choose to "live by the flesh," find moral restraint a burden. However, those who obey Christ's two great positive commandments—to love God and love their neighbor—find in God's law the fundamental and necessary way to practice love and to live a wholesome Christian life.[14]

The second chapter of the encyclical examines the contemporary disorder that the pope identifies as the false belief that individual freedom inevitably opposes moral law. Modern culture tends to "exalt freedom to such an extent that it becomes an absolute, breeding an individualism that denies the very existence of human nature and the moral limits intrinsic to it." In his third chapter, John Paul II discusses the importance of martyrdom. As a teacher of "unchanging moral norms," the Church is not the enemy of particular cultures, but at their service. In serving, however, the Church must give a "clear and forceful presentation of moral truth," often contradicting prevailing beliefs. The pope concluded his piece warning that despite the fall of totalitarian Marxism, "there is no less grave a danger that fundamental rights will be denied today," and "that the religious yearnings arising in the heart of every human being will be absorbed once again into politics." Finally, the pope cautions against living in a "democracy [that] without values easily turns into open or thinly disguised totalitarianism."[15]

While it was John Paul II's hope that *Veritatis Splendor* would inspire unity within the Church, the document created as much dissension as solidarity among the clergy and laity. Since the reforms of Vatican II, many bishops had embraced theologies in which moral law was seen as more subjective than objective. They saw moral law more as a helpful tool, rather than as something that is eternally binding. As the archbishop of Vancouver described it: "Our problem today is that we no longer seek freedom in truth. What we now demand is freedom from truth."[16]

Others saw the encyclical differently. Hans Küng, the Swiss theologian whom the pope had earlier chastised, stated defiantly that in writing *Veritatis Splendor*, the pope had made his personal beliefs Catholic doctrine. Accusing the pope of "messianism," Küng stated that the encyclical was more an admission of failure in that modern Catholics by and large were not following many of the current teachings of the Church. The pope was desperate, Küng concluded, for the Church was losing its hold over the faithful. Others were more circumspect in their criticism: "The encyclical says the right things," complained one bishop, "but what are we supposed to do with it? Our job is to find a way to bring people back into the churches."[17]

MAN OF THE YEAR

The year 1994 was particularly busy for the pope. It was full of great triumphs and terrible sadness. Two journeys, one to Beirut, Lebanon, the other to Sarajevo, Bosnia, were canceled because of the hostilities. In Rwanda, where 60 percent of the population is Catholic, thousands of persons were massacred as a result of tribal conflicts. This tragedy saddened John Paul II. But amid the upheaval of world affairs, John Paul II appeared to be making some headway. The Catechism of the Catholic Church appeared in an English translation, the first such document since the sixteenth century. The book, while criticized by some clergy as being tedious and unreadable, summarizes the essential beliefs and moral tenets of the Church. The book also included a list of new "sins," including tax evasion, drug abuse, mistreatment of immigrants, abuse of the environment, and genetic engineering. Some believe that the Catechism will be one of the most enduring milestones of John Paul II's papacy. The pope also achieved a personal goal with the establishment of diplomatic relations with Israel, ending a standoff of almost fifty years.

In May, the pope issued an apostolic letter in which he definitively refused to allow women to enter the priesthood. His imperious response angered Catholics worldwide. Many believed that the pope's narrow interpretation of Church teachings was in fact a missed opportunity to explain why this particular policy must still be maintained. To critics, missed opportunities followed John Paul II throughout his papacy.

But the biggest uproar came in September at a United Nations conference on population in Cairo, Egypt, where representatives from 185 nations and the Vatican met. One of the central items of the conference was a 113-page plan asking governments to commit $17 billion annually by the year 2000 to curb population growth. At the time of the conference, almost 90 percent of the document had been approved. It was the remaining 10 percent that the pope was most concerned about.

Among the most controversial portions of the plan was Paragraph 8.25, which was inserted by the Clinton administration. The clause stated that "the United States believes access to safe, legal, and voluntary abortion is a fundamental right of all women."[18] The American delegation asked that the conference endorse the clause.

Although the pope was not present at the conference, he had been keeping in close contact with his representatives. When he learned of the proposed clause, he became concerned, and as one Vatican spokesman wrote, "He feared for the first time in the history of humanity, abortion was being proposed as a means of population control."[19] For the next nine days, the Vatican delegation lobbied to defeat the proposed clause, working with delegates from Latin American and Islamic countries who also opposed abortion. The pope won, and the clause was replaced with a statement that "in no case should abortion be promoted as a method of family planning."[20] In return, the Vatican gave partial consent to the document.

But the victory was costly for the pope. One Spanish critic called the pope "a traveling salesman of demographic irrationality," while Hans Küng declared, "This pope is a disaster for our church." For those watching the contest of wills, it was simply the pope at work. The Cairo conference also served as a perfect illustration of what John Paul II's papacy has been all about: "the problem of the Pope in a modern world and the problem the Pope has with the modern world."[21]

Two events that occurred during 1994 helped intensify the somewhat strange celebrity status of the pope: the publication of his book *Crossing the Threshold of Hope,* and being named *Time* magazine's "Man of the Year." As for the pope's seeming inability to meet his detractors halfway, one priest noted, "He's the one keeping these issues alive, things people should reflect on morally."[22] Both the publication of his book and designation as "Man of the Year" gave the pope additional forums to reach people all over the world.

Crossing the Threshold of Hope was done in conjunction with publishers in 35 countries and was the first book written by a reigning pontiff for the general public. American publisher Alfred A. Knopf paid $8.5 million for publication rights, which became one of the highest amounts paid for a single volume published in the United States. The October release of the book was to coincide with John Paul II's arrival in New York at the start of a four-city U.S. tour, but the pope canceled the visit due to hip-replacement surgery that April. By the end of the year, the book had sold five million copies, 1.5 million of those in the United States, and had been printed in 20 languages. The book reiterates John Paul's teachings on a variety of subjects, including the existence of God, pain and suffering, eternal life, the relationship of Christianity to other religions, and a hope for Christian unity. The pope was expected to earn tens of millions of dollars in royalties from the book, but he has said he would donate the money to charity.

While the book was a publishing sensation, John Paul II by this time, had at least four books of homilies, devotional reflections, and essays published. None of those works were received with such fanfare as *Crossing the Threshold of Hope*. Part of what made the book different was the manner in which it came about. To mark the 15th anniversary of his pontificate in October 1993, something truly unprecedented was planned. It was agreed that John Paul II was going to give an extended television interview that would be broadcast simultaneously around the world. The plan was later tabled. But the pope still had the questions that Vittorio Messori, the scheduled interviewer for the broadcast, had intended to ask him. Instead of completely shelving the project, the pope, using the questions, from time to time jotted down his responses. Topics covered in the book included the existence of God, the importance of young people in the Church, the promise of the future, and the nature of suffering. While some critics found the book a rehashing of ideas that the pope has expressed through the years, others found the book refreshing, thoughtful, and accessible.

However, the pope did not escape completely unscathed from this experience. Describing the Buddhist religion in his book as "negative" and "atheist" earned him a bitter and searing reprisal from members of the Buddhist community. Complaining that the pope was nothing more than a bigoted colonialist, Buddhist and other critics forced the pope to issue clarifications in which he stated that he had meant nothing demeaning, but was merely making a theological point. But the damage had been done, and during the pope's 1995 trip to Sri Lanka, many of the Buddhists boycotted papal events.

Not more than two months after the publication of *Crossing the Threshold of Hope*, the pope was in the public eye once again as *Time's* "Man of the Year." Reporters tried to describe what it is about the pope that made him revered as a popular hero and influential spiritual leader:

> His appearances generate an electricity unmatched by anyone else on earth. That explains, for instance, why in rural Kenyan villages thousands of children, plus many cats and roosters and even hotels, are named John Paul. Charisma is the only conceivable reason why a CD featuring him saying the rosary—in Latin—against a background of Bach and Handel is currently ascending the charts in Europe. It also accounts for the dazed reaction of a young woman who found herself, along with the thousands around her in a sports stadium in Denver, cheering and applauding him: "I don't react that way to rock groups. What is it that he has?"[23]

THE CULTURE OF DEATH

On March 30, 1995, Pope John Paul II issued his 11th encyclical, *Evangelium Vitae*, "The Gospel of Life," which also became the first encyclical available on the Internet. The document was drawn up in response to a request from a group of cardinals in Rome four years earlier. As the pope later wrote: "The cardinals unanimously asked me to reaffirm with the authority of the Successor of Peter the value of human life and its inviolability, in the light of present circumstances and attacks threatening it today."[24]

Evangelium Vitae is John Paul II's dark vision of the modern age. In it, the pope challenges modern humanity's quest to maximize individual freedoms, while demonstrating how the issues of abortion, contraception, and capital punishment are connected with his vision of a "culture of death." This "culture of death" is in itself an important contradiction. On the one hand, there is a growing sensitivity to the rights and dignities of human beings as seen in the declarations of human rights of many nations. But, on the other hand, some of the very same nations reject such rights in practice, through the use of capital punishment, euthanasia, torture, and false imprisonment.

While *Evangelium Vitae* breaks little new ground, it does clearly spell out the Church's longstanding opposition to abortion and euthanasia. John Paul II also expressed the view that capital punishment can rarely, if ever, be justified in the modern age. The encyclical rejects artificial means of contraception, methods of artificial reproduction, most embryo research, and the use of prenatal diagnostic tests as a pretense for what the pope called "eugenic abortion."[25] While the Catholic Church has long voiced its opposition to abortion and euthanasia, this is the first time that the opposition has been given the weight of an encyclical. Predictably, the new document drew praise from conservative Catholics and indifference from critics of the Church and the pope.

ISSUES OF APOLOGY

The pope might appear incapable of admitting wrongdoing on the part of the Church, but during the 1990s John Paul II, acting on behalf of the Church, redressed mistakes that the Church had made throughout history. One of the most startling admissions came in 1992, when the pope acknowledged that the Church had been wrong in condemning the Italian scientist Galileo for his theory that the Earth revolved around the sun. While the Church long realized that it had been wrong, the pope was the first to admit publicly the mistake.

In 1994, the pope wrote a 27-page letter to his cardinals asking them to rethink the position the Church had taken on other historical errors. Among the possibilities the pope considered were religious wars that were fought by or on behalf of the Church, which had caused "inexcusable violence and death."[26] Among other events to reconsider was the Inquisition, in which thousands had died at the hands of the Church or as victims of Catholic anti-Semitic campaigns. In 1996, the pope went so far as to acknowledge that it was possible for a world where evolution and creationism could coexist. The pope also admitted the Church had been wrong in not doing more to save the Jews during the Holocaust of World War II.

A DRAMATIC TRIP

In 1998, Pope John Paul II made one of his most dramatic and reward-ing journeys when he traveled to Cuba, the last bastion of Soviet-style communism. Upon his arrival in Havana, the pope proclaimed, "Cuba must open to the world and the world must open to Cuba."[27] His belief was that peaceful change can occur only when Cuba is no longer isolated from the world; and when economic and diplomatic restrictions such as the U.S. embargo and unfriendly treatment at the hands of fellow Latin American governments are gone. Similarly, the country would open up from the inside once the restrictions put in place by the Castro regime were also undone. John Paul II also believed that Latin American coun-tries that were pro-democracy would help Cuba make this transition.

Arriving in January, the Pope had to forego his traditional kiss of the ground because of his physical ailments. Instead, four children dressed in white, held up a tray of Cuban soil for the pope to kiss. Even Fidel Castro, usually seen in the olive fatigues that are the uniform of his revolution, wore a dark blue suit to greet the pope. For Castro, the papal visit was a gamble, as he hoped to use it as an opportunity to improve his image around the world, as well as to change American policy toward Cuba.

The pope's trip was a five-day whirlwind. As a visibly frail John Paul II traveled the length of the island to conduct four outdoor Masses, he at-tracted a mix of Catholic believers eager for a papal blessing and those merely curious to see the pope. In public homilies, his aim was to stimu-late new, even revolutionary ideas within Castro's closed society. Yet his message, unlike those given to Poles during his historic visit in 1979, was more religious than political, as the pope lectured against the loss of fam-ily values rather than the country's lack of human rights. The pope also spoke on issues that were of particular relevance to Cubans, such as abor-tion, divorce, and premarital sex. John Paul II criticized both the U.S. em-bargo and communist ideology, but in gentler tones than he might have used earlier. In response, Castro did agree to free some political prisoners, but refused to allow more priests, parochial schools, or freer media access in Cuba.

THE MILLENNIUM POPE

As of 2003, the pope continues to make his way. He is older now, and his physical condition has deteriorated markedly over the years. His last skiing trip was years ago; a series of falls led to hip replacement surgery, while aftereffects of the assassin's bullet in 1981 have also contributed to a series of various ailments, such as fevers and stomach pains. The pope also suffers from Parkinson's disease, an affliction that affects the nervous system, causing uncontrollable shaking and mental disorders. He no longer strides down the massive halls of the Vatican, but instead rides in an electric cart to get to where he needs to go.

The pope's seemingly fragile health has given rise to rumors that he will step down. But those close to him dismiss that suggestion. The pope will continue to be the pope until he dies. Still, Vatican officials must now consider the question of what to do if the pope becomes incapacitated, and there has been some talk of implementing a policy that would provide direction should that situation arise.

While the pope's health may be deteriorating, his mind remains sharp. When the Church was rocked in 2002 by a series of sexual misconduct cases involving clergy who had molested children, the pope called a special meeting of cardinals and bishops in Rome to address the problem. When some cardinals suggested that perhaps it was time to change the celibacy requirement for priests, the pope refused, stating that "The priesthood must never be seen as a means for improving one's lot in life or in terms of gaining prestige."[28] But he did agree that the Church needed to be more direct in its dealings with sexual misconduct cases, and to work harder to attract priests who do not pose such dangers to the Catholic community.

A DAY IN THE LIFE

Pope John Paul II's life has changed little since he came to the Vatican. Until the mid-1990s, he arose every morning at 5:30; now he awakens every day at 5 A.M. By 6:15, he is in his private chapel where he prays and meditates for two hours. Sometimes he lies prostrate in front of the altar; at other times he kneels at his wooden prie-dieu, or kneeler, with eyes closed, his forehead cradled in his left hand. The pope's prie-dieu has a padded armrest, which, when lifted, holds a small container for prayer books and stacks of yellow sheets of paper that have prayer intentions (prayers for specific people or events) scribbled on them.

After his morning prayers, the pope celebrates Mass, to which special guests have been invited, often local priests and people from around Rome. Afterward, the pope has breakfast with his guests. He then walks to his study where he works alone until 11 A.M. While there, the pope reads, writes, and attends to the daily business of his office. When possible, he writes in Polish using a black felt-tipped pen. Lately, because of his health, he dictates his thoughts, so that they can later be transcribed by one of his secretaries. After the morning's work, the pope holds private audiences in which he meets with groups and individuals.

Lunch is usually served at 2 P.M., with the pope dining with bishops and other Church officials. Following his doctor's orders, the pope takes a short rest for about half an hour after lunch. If his hip is not bothering him too much, he will take a walk on the roof terrace of the Vatican. Then it's back to work in his study until 6:30, where he receives Vatican officials for discussion of Church matters. If time allows, the pope usually tries to see Polish visitors when they come.

Dinner is always served at 8 P.M., and is usually spent with friends or close aides at the Vatican. If dining with Vatican officials, the meal is served family style where the food is passed around the table with each person helping himself. For more formal dinners, the pope's valet, wearing a waiter's jacket, serves the meal. Often the menu features Italian cuisine, with pasta or antipasto served first, followed by a meat dish with vegetables and salad. Fruit with cheese or a Polish pastry is served for dessert. When a French cardinal was asked whether the pope's meals were any good, the cardinal replied, "Coming from Lyons, that's hard for me to say—but there are a sufficient number of calories."[29]

The pope sees mealtime—particularly dinner—as an opportunity to converse, debate, and bounce ideas around. His mastery of eight languages allows him to converse with most anyone who comes to his dinner table. He is also known to sing and joke with his company. Often he is seen pushing his food around, or fiddling with his cutlery, all the while paying close attention to his dinner companions' conversation. At the dinner's conclusion, the pope returns to his study once more to work and pray. He seldom is in bed much before midnight.

The pope is attended to by five black-robed nuns from the Polish order of the Servants of the Sacred Heart who cook his meals and take care of his laundry. He is also attended by a valet and two personal secretaries, Monsignor Stanislaw Dziwisz, who is Polish, and Monsignor Vincent Tran Ngoc Thu, who is Vietnamese. Monsignor Dziwisz also serves as the pope's "gatekeeper." No one sees the Holy Father without first securing Dziwisz's approval.

When not at work or prayer, the pope enjoys reading books on history, philosophy, and sociology. He also reads serious literature and poetry, often in its original language; he is particularly fond of Russian literature and the poetry of German poet Rainer Maria Rilke. The pope rarely watches television except for an occasional soccer game. He reads one newspaper faithfully: a weekly Catholic newspaper from Kraków. To keep up with the staggering amount of current events every day, the pope relies on news summaries prepared by aides to the Vatican Secretary of State. Every Friday the pope meets with Cardinal Ratzinger, who serves as head theologian for the Church, to discuss Vatican affairs, while Saturdays are reserved for meetings with the head of the Congregation of Bishops, where the two discuss appointments of various individuals to the high of-fices of the Church, such as archbishops or cardinals. He also confesses his sins and receives absolution from a Polish priest who has known the pope for many years.

A SIMPLE LIFE

Compared to the sumptuous and majestic splendors of the Vatican, the pope's apartment is quite simple. His living quarters consist of an office that is shared by the two secretaries, a chapel, a dining room, large and small reception rooms, and the pope's private office and bedroom. The bedroom is divided in two, separated by an old-fashioned folding screen. On one side is a desk, on the other, a full-size bed with a white bedspread, several freestanding closets, and a large table on which rest several large books of photography that the pope enjoys looking at. On one wall of the bedroom is a map of the diocese of Rome, where pins have been placed in-dicating the parishes the pope has visited. There are only two photo-graphs throughout the pope's private quarters. One is a small photograph of the pope's mentor, Cardinal Adam Sapieha, which is found in the pope's office. The other is a small wedding photograph of his parents, rest-ing on a table in his bedroom.

OLD FRIENDS

The pope has worked hard at maintaining his own personal sphere, separate from that of his work. Unlike other popes, John Paul II does not ask permission to keep in touch with friends old and new; he simply does it. When he wants to invite friends to spend time with him at Castel Gan-dolfo, the papal summer retreat, he bypasses the Vatican secretaries and extends the invitation himself.

He also has kept in touch with his friends from Poland. Several times a year he dines with his old childhood friend, Jerzy Kluger, who became a businessman in Rome. Kluger also is one of the few people who still can call his old friend "Lolek." When he was in better health, the pope's con-stant hiking companion was Father Tadeusz Styczen, a philosophy profes-sor from the University of Lublin. Friends from the Rhapsodic Theater who wrote to their old friend have always had every letter answered. As one actress commented, "It's intimidating really, you can't write nonsense to the Pope when you know that, no matter what, he's going to take time out to write back to you. The responses aren't long, and they aren't always handwritten.... I think of him as a man who needs to stay in touch with his friends because he is so terribly busy."[30]

The pope continues to travel, though not as much as before. In 2002, he has journeyed to Bulgaria, Africa, and Canada, to attend a World Youth Day gathering in Toronto. He also plans to visit Mexico, Guatemala, and Poland. In his time as pope, he has visited over 140 countries, making him the most-traveled pope in history. He has also met 510 heads of state, 150 prime ministers, and has created 137 cardinals.

His successes are an important indication of how John Paul II has used the office of the papacy. He was instrumental in helping bring about the collapse of communism in his homeland, and helped set in motion the ensuing disintegration of Soviet rule throughout Eastern Europe. He demonstrated, through the power of words and faith, how totalitarian governments can not only be weakened, but defeated. Observers are still watching to see the results of his 1998 visit to Cuba.

But in his battle with the forces of the modern world the pope has not emerged as the clear victor. Part of the problem is the pope's own limitations in understanding how democratic institutions function. Because of that, his view of the Western world, particularly the United States, has been clouded and has cost him a vital audience.

One theme remains constant for the pope: the importance of revering the human spirit and the sanctity of the individual life, particularly those unable to take care of themselves or who, because they have not been favored with wealth or status, suffer the indignities of being forgotten and abused. But the pope is facing a difficult time; while many Catholics around the world may applaud his courageous stand on difficult issues, they still walk away from the Church. To John Paul II, this is only a call to stand fast and take heart in the motto that has guided him all his life: "Be not afraid." In those three words, a single man has taken on the challenges of a centuries-old institution, a modern world, and all that goes with both. He has forever changed the nature of what it means to be pope, and neither the world nor the Catholic Church will ever be the same.

NOTES

1. Carl Bernstein and Marco Politi, *His Holiness: John Paul II and the Hidden History of Our Time* (New York: Doubleday, 1996), p. 492.

2. Ibid.

3. Ibid., p. 493.

4. Jonathan Kwitney, *Man of the Century: The Life and Times of Pope John Paul II* (New York: Henry Holt, 1997), p. 623.

5. Bernstein and Politi, p. 496.

6. Ibid.

7. Kwitney, p. 614.

8. Ibid., p. 318.

9. Ibid., p. 618.

10. Ibid., p. 634.

11. John Paul II, *Crossing the Threshold of Hope,* edited by Vittorio Messori (New York: Alfred A. Knopf, 1994), p. 125.

12. Kwitney, p. 642.

13. Joe Woodard, "A Most Misunderstood Message" *Alberta Report/Newsmagazine* 20, no. 45 (25 October 1993): p. 38.

14. Ibid.

15. Ibid.

16. Ibid.

17. Bernstein and Politi, p. 505.

18. Paul Gray and Thomas Sancton, "Man of the Year," *Time*, 26 December 1994, p. 48+.

19. Ibid.

20. Ibid.

21. Ibid.

22. Ibid.

23. Ibid.

24. Richard A. McCormick, "The Gospel of Life," *America* 172, no. 15 (29 April 1995): 10+.

25. "Pope Decries 'Culture of Death,' " *Christian Century* 112, no. 12 (12 April 1995): 384–385.

26. Robert Andreas, ed., *Pope John Paul II: A Tribute* (Boston: Bulfinch Press, 1999), p. 119.

27. Tad Szulc, "John Paul II and Cuba," *America* 181, no. 19 (11 December 1999): 6+.

28. "Pontiff Addressed Scandals," *Richmond Times Dispatch,* 21 April 2002, p. 1.

29. John Elson and Greg Burke, "Lives of the Pope," *Time*, 26 December 1994, p. 60+.

30. Ibid.

BIBLIOGRAPHY

Andreas, Robert, ed. *Pope John Paul II: A Tribute*. Boston: Bulfinch Press, 1999.

Barnes, Jane. "Frontline: The Millennial Pope," accessed June 10, 2002, located at: http://www.pbs.org/wgbh/pages/frontline/shows/pope/etc/bio2.html.

Baum, Gregory. "The Impact of John Paul's Social Teaching." *Ecumenism* 79 (September 1985): 23–24.

———. "The Impact of Marxism on the Thought of John Paul II." *Thought* 62 (March 1987): 26–38.

Bernstein, Carl and Marco Politi. *His Holiness: John Paul II and the Hidden History of Our Time*. New York: Doubleday, 1996.

Elson, John and Greg Burke. "Lives of the Pope." *Time*, 26 December 1994, p. 60+.

Gray, Paul and Thomas Sancton. "Man of the Year." *Time*, 26 December 1994, p. 48+.

Hebblethwaite, Peter. "Understanding Pope Wojtyla." *IDOC Bulletin* 11–12 (1982): 3–5.

———. "The Mind of John Paul II." *Grail* 1 (March 1985): 19–33.

John Paul II. *Be Not Afraid: Pope John Paul II Speaks Out on His Life, His Beliefs, and His Inspiring Vision for Humanity*. New York: St. Martin's Press, 1984.

———. *Crossing the Threshold of Hope*. Edited by Vittorio Messori. New York: Alfred A. Knopf, 1994.

———. *Fear Not: Thoughts on Living in Today's World*. Edited by Alexandra Hatcher. New York: Andrews McMeel, 1999.

———. *Gift and Mystery: On the Fiftieth Anniversary of My Priestly Ordination*. New York: Doubleday, 1996.

————. *The Place Within: The Poetry of John Paul II*. New York: Random House, 1994.

Johnson, Douglas. "Heaven and Earth through the Eyes of the Pope." *Washington Post*, 21–27 November 1994, national weekly edition, p. 35.

Johnson, Paul. *Pope John Paul II and the Catholic Restoration*. Ann Arbor, MI: Servant Books, 1981.

Kohn, Hans. "The Crisis of European Thought and Culture." In *World War I: A Turning Point in Modern History*, ed. Jack Roth. New York: Alfred A. Knopf, 1967, p. 28.

Kwitney, Jonathan. *Man of the Century: The Life and Times of Pope John Paul II*. New York: Henry Holt, 1997.

Langan, John. "Order and Justice under John Paul II." *Christian Century* 97 (30 April 1980): 493–498.

Lukacs, John. *The End of the Twentieth Century and the End of the Modern Age*. New York: Ticknor and Fields, 1993, p. 205.

McCormick, Richard A. "The Gospel of Life." *America* 172, no. 15 (29 April 1995).

Neuhaus, Richard John. "The Mind of the Most Powerful Man in the World: John Paul II: Philosopher and Pope." *Worldview* 24 (September 1981): 11–13.

O'Brien, Darcy. *The Hidden Pope*. New York: Rodale Press, 1998.

"The Papal Years: Charisma and Restoration," accessed December 4, 2001, located at: http://www.cnn.com/SPECIALS/1999/pope/bio/papal/index.html.

"Pontiff Addressed Scandals." *Richmond Times Dispatch*, 21 April 2002, 1.

"Pope Decries 'Culture of Death,'" *Christian Century* 112, no. 12 (12 April 1995): 384–385.

Quade, Quentin L., ed. *The Pope and Revolution: John Paul II Confronts Liberation Theology*. Washington, D.C.: Ethics and Public Policy Center, 1982.

Schall, James V. "Liberation in John Paul II." In *Liberation Theology in Latin America*, ed. James V. Schall. San Francisco: Ignatius Press, 1982, pp. 104–121.

"The Social Teachings of Pope John Paul II." *Social Thought* 13 (spring-summer 1987): 6–167.

Sullivan, Robert. *Pope John Paul II: A Tribute*. New York: Time, 1999.

Szulc, Tad. *Pope John Paul II: The Biography*. New York: Scribner, 1995.

————. "John Paul II and Cuba." *America* 181, no. 19 (11 December 1999): 6+.

————. *Witness to Hope: The Biography of John Paul II*. New York: Harper Collins, 1999.

Weigel, George. *The Final Revolution*. New York: Oxford University Press, 1992.

Willey, David. *God's Politician: Pope John Paul II, the Catholic Church, and the New World Order*. New York: St. Martin's Press, 1992.

Williams, George Huntston. *The Mind of John Paul II: Origins of His Thought and Action*. New York: Seabury Press, 1981.

Wills, Garry. *Why I Am a Catholic*. New York: Houghton Mifflin, 2002.

Woodard, Joe. "A Most Misunderstood Message." *Alberta Report/Newsmagazine* 20, no. 45 (25 October 1993): 38.

INDEX

About the Author

MEG GREENE is a freelance writer. She has written numerous biographies of historical and popular culture figures.